FIRST FOR BOYS

The Boys' Brigade

Patron
Her Majesty The Queen

————————————————

————————————————

————————————————

————————————————

————————————————

————————————————

————————————————

————————————————

W . HADDEN

FIRST FOR BOYS

The Story of The Boys' Brigade
1883–1983

Donald M. McFarlan

COLLINS

Glasgow & London

Published by William Collins Sons and Company Limited
Text copyright © 1982 Donald M. McFarlan
Illustrations copyright © 1982 The Boys' Brigade
First published 1982

Typeset by Coats Dataprint, Inverness
Printed in Great Britain by Collins Glasgow

ISBN 0 00 434279 8

THE BOYS' BRIGADE

BRIGADE HOUSE, PARSONS GREEN, LONDON, SW6 4TH
TELEPHONE: 01-736 8481   TELEGRAMS: EDAGIRB, LONDON, SW6

"THE ADVANCEMENT OF CHRIST'S KINGDOM AMONG BOYS, AND THE PROMOTION OF HABITS OF OBEDIENCE, REVERENCE, DISCIPLINE, SELF-RESPECT, AND ALL THAT TENDS TOWARDS A TRUE CHRISTIAN MANLINESS"

"Our Ancestors, of whom we should oft read,
And hold in mind their noble worthy deed,
We let overslide, through very slothfulness,
And cast us ever to other business".

There words are obviously ancient, and indeed they are.
The Scottish poet known as "Blind Harry" wrote them
some 500 years ago, when he told the tale of the illustrious
and valiant champion, Sir William Wallace. Today, Doctor
McFarlan has taken our story and set it down with warm
friendship. We can see more than one illustrious and noble
man as the years pass: but they all champion one Object.
We also appear different from our Founders; things of which
they never dreamed are ours for normal use; but our Object
is the same. This story reminds us of our start and shows
us the business which is ours to do today.

Elgin.

Preface

This book is for the B.B. Boys of yesterday, today and tomorrow. The Boys of yesterday will recall many of the events described here, perhaps through rose-coloured spectacles! The Boys of today must make the Brigade of tomorrow, and the Boys of the new and unknown B.B. century should be proud to learn of their roots.

I have had much help in writing this book from many B.B. men and women at Brigade House in London and in Glasgow and throughout the Movement. In particular I must mention the constant encouragement given me by John M. Leggat (former Secretary of the Glasgow Battalion), John R. Edbrooke, (Secretary for Development), Muriel D. Ellis (Brigade archivist) and the Brigade Secretary, Alfred Hudson.

This book is but a glimpse of the Movement which was and is 'First For Boys'. It is sent out with good wishes to the Movement of which I am proud to be a member.

Donald McFarlan

CONTENTS

THE BOYS' BRIGADE
FIRST FOR BOYS

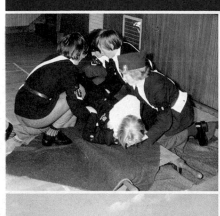

The Boys' Brigade was founded in Glasgow on Thursday 4th October, 1883. It was the first of all the uniformed organizations for boys and girls which have since spread all over the world.

Glasgow was proud to call itself the second city of the Empire. It was the age of progress, a time of invention, of building machines and making things. Queen Victoria had reigned for nearly fifty glorious years, and her Empire was still expanding. The prosperity of the second city was at its peak. It was claimed that almost every manufactured article in the world was made somewhere in Glasgow – in the smoking factories, chemical works, dyeworks, foundries, machine shops – or shipped from her warehouses by way of the River Clyde to the furthest corners of the earth. Glasgow was the greatest place in the world for locomotives, and four out of every five ocean-going ships were built on the Clyde.

Factories and offices opened at seven in the morning and closed at six in the evening. Shops remained open until nine or ten at night. It was a busy, bustling city all through the working week.

Sunday was different. Old Scottish custom brought complete peace to the city every Sunday morning. Perhaps less then twenty per cent of the population went to church, but the ministers and magistrates saw to it that there was a decent and holy calm. There were more than thirty denominations of the Church in Glasgow and well over three hundred church buildings and meeting places.

It was a business man, part-time soldier and loyal churchman, William A. Smith, who founded The Boys' Brigade.

William Alexander Smith was twenty-nine years of age. He was born on 27th October, 1854 at Pennyland, near Thurso, on the stormy north-east coast of Scotland. His father and his grandfather before him had been officers in the Army. When young William came south to Glasgow at the age of nearly fifteen it was to begin work as clerk in his uncle Fraser's soft goods business. While he was still in his teens he enrolled in the 1st Lanarkshire Rifle Volunteers, and a year later he became a member of the Free College Church, near his uncle's and aunts' home in the fashionable west end of the city.

Young William filled every hour of every day of the week with work, drill parade, and church meetings. Indeed, his uncle grumbled a bit about his enthusiasm for soldiering, and complained that he was never at home. In those martial and imperial days it was customary for young men of spirit to join the Volunteers. After all, the British Army fought more than a hundred wars and frontier engagements throughout the Empire in those years of 'Hope and Glory'. William

SURE AND STEDFAST

The Founder in 1883

The First Lanark Rifles Gazette.

No. 1, Vol. I.]   TUESDAY, 16TH NOV., 1886.   [PRICE TWOPENCE.

CONTENTS.

Regimental Gathering and Presentation of Prizes,

THEATRE ROYAL, GLASGOW,

TUESDAY EVENING, 16th NOVEMBER, 1886.

PROGRAMME.

7-30 to 8 P.M.—2ND BATTALION BAND, BANDMASTER HOWELL, *Conductor.*

1.—OVERTURE, ... "In Memoriam," ... *Newton.*
2.—SELECTION, ... "The Bohemian Girl," ... *Balfe.*
3.—VALSE, ... "Mikado," ... *Bucalossi.*

8 P.M.—WALTZ, ... "Verena," *Composed by* Private MARSHALL F. REID, 1ST L.R.V.
1ST BATTALION BAND (ADAMS'), *Conductor,* H. J. O'NEIL.
DUMB-BELL EXERCISES, ... MEMBERS OF THE 1ST L.R.V.A.A.C.
INDIAN CLUB EXERCISES, ... Sergeant-Major CANSDALE.
8-10 P.M.—VOCAL MUSIC, ... MEMBERS OF GLEE CLUB.
8-20 P.M.—OVERTURE, ... "Merry Wives of Windsor," ... *Nicolai.*
1ST BATTALION BAND.

8-30. p.m.—PRESENTATION OF PRIZES.

The names of Prize-winners entitled to appear will be found Marked * in Lists on Pages 7 and 8.

9-0 P.M.—GRAND SELECTION, ... "Mefistofele," ... *Boito.*
1ST BATTALION BAND.
SWORD FEATS, by Sergeant-Major CANSDALE, Instructor, Gymnasium, Maryhill Barracks.
WALTZ, ... "Soiree d'Eté," ... *Waldteufel.*
1ST BATTALION BAND.
HORIZONTAL BAR EXERCISES, ... MEMBERS OF 1ST L.R.V.A.A.C.
9-20 P.M.—FANTASIA, ... "The Jacobite," ... *Gassner.*
1ST BATTALION BAND.
With Solos for Clarionet, Cornet, and Euphonium—Messrs. GREEN, HILL, and MERRET.
9-35 P.M.—FARCE, "A Waltz by Arditi," by JOHN OXENFORD, Characters by the MEMBERS OF THE
1ST L.R.V. DRAMATIC SOCIETY.
10-10 P.M.—VOCAL MUSIC, ... MEMBERS OF GLEE CLUB.

GOD SAVE THE QUEEN.

Smith was tall, manly and military in bearing, and it was natural that he should want to follow in his father's and grandfather's footsteps. His other main interest was with some of his friends in the YMCA. And it may be noted in passing that by the time he was eighteen he was already friendly with the girl who was later to be his wife.

The minister of the Free College Church was the Reverend George Reith (father of Lord Reith who became the first Director-General of the BBC). William Smith became a teacher in the Sabbath School

1st Lanarkshire Rifle Volunteers
'Mounted Detachment' with
William A. Smith

which was held in a mission hall in North Woodside Road, not far from the church. It was in the Sabbath School that he struck a snag, and had an idea. The snag was that the older boys were bored and restless. No one seemed able to interest or control them. They felt they were too old for the Sabbath School and they were suspicious of 'do-gooders' and teachers who told them to sit still, make less noise, and generally behave themselves. In short, they were typical healthy teenagers.

Smith thought a lot about it. On a Saturday afternoon, as an enthusiastic young officer in the Volunteers, he had no difficulty in making a hundred men obey his every word of command on the nearby drill ground. Yet on a Sunday he could do nothing with a small group of lively boys. It was then he had his idea: 'Drill and Discipline'. Why not turn his Sabbath School boys into a volunteer band or brigade, with the same military order, obedience, discipline and self-respect as any well-trained corps of the Army of the Queen? Religious instruction was the core of Sabbath School work. But why should not the boys enjoy games as well as discipline, gymnastics and sport as well as hymns and prayers?

William Smith discussed his ideas with two of his close friends in the YMCA, the brothers James R. Hill and John B. Hill who taught in the Sabbath School with him and who were fellow Volunteers. Nothing was left to chance. The programme was talked out with care for every detail and, with their plans made, they asked God's blessing on it. Later, William Smith was to sum up his aims in these words:

> The aim was to devise something that would appeal to a boy on the heroic side of his nature – something that would let him see that in the service of God there is as much scope for all that is brave and true and manly as in the service of King and Country.

On 4th October 1883 the three leaders invited the boys of North Woodside Mission Sabbath School to join *The Boys' Brigade*. The badge was to be an anchor and the motto: 'Sure and Stedfast'. William Smith took the words and the spelling and the crest from the Authorized Version of the Epistle to the Hebrews, chapter 6, verse 19: 'Which hope we have as an anchor of the soul, both sure and stedfast'. Name and badge and motto remain through the hundred years since that momentous day. The Object was also quite clear from the beginning:

> The advancement of Christ's Kingdom among Boys and the promotion of habits of Reverence, Discipline, Self-Respect, and all that tends towards a true Christian Manliness.

(The word Obedience was added some ten years later).

It was typical of William Smith's serious purpose, and true to the spirit of the times, that he put down all the important words with a capital letter. Throughout its history the most important person in the B.B. has always been The Boy.

As yet there was no uniform, but the leaders wore a small red rosette in their lapels. Fifty-nine boys volunteered to join right away, some out of curiosity, others ready to see what fun they could make of the new idea. All of them were between the ages of 12 and 16. When they learned that 'discipline' meant what was said, the number of recruits dropped to 35. From the very beginning William Smith was as strict with his Boys as the Army had taught him to be with himself and his Volunteers. One of the first rules was that no Boy was allowed to 'fall in' if he were even a minute late on parade at eight o'clock, and

another made it clear that 'no member was allowed to miss two drills running'.

North Woodside Mission Hall where the B.B. began

The story of The Boys' Brigade has spread a popular myth that William Smith formed his first company from ragged, barefoot urchins who hung about the slum streets of Glasgow. This is quite untrue. The Boys of the 1st Glasgow Company came from the homes of skilled artisans and craftsmen in the prospering north-west of the city. This was to be a feature in the growth of the B.B. in other cities up and down the land in the early days. It should be remembered that boys could leave school and go to work at the age of 12 in those days; William Smith himself had left school when he was only 14. Half of the members of the original company already had jobs as apprentice joiners, cabinet-makers, blacksmiths, clerks, or engine fitters. No doubt they had to work long hours, even on a Saturday night, but Smith noted with pride that they were keen enough to turn up for

15

Bible Class at 9.30 a.m. prompt on a Sunday, with or without breakfast.

The year 1883 closed with an examination for promotion among the Boys. After careful consideration of drill, written work, conduct and character, two sergeants, two corporals and two lance-corporals were appointed, and the Company was divided under them into six squads. The 1st Glasgow Company of the Boys' Brigade was well and truly established.

————————

Mode of addressing Officers and Boys:

'For purposes of correspondence, Officers of the Brigade should not be addressed by military titles, except by the Boys. Letters to Boys should always be addressed according to their rank, as Sergeant——, Private——, etc. The term "Master" suggests a higher social grade than most of our Boys move in, while "Mr" applied to a small Boy of 12 is obviously absurd.'

William A. Smith

Within a year the Boys of the 1st Glasgow were in uniform. Although the leaders might have liked to see the Boys as smartly turned out as their Volunteers on parade, William Smith wisely set his face against full uniform clothing. It would be too expensive for one thing, whereas cap, belt and haversack cost only eighteen pence (about 7½p. in modern money).

It is interesting to guess where Smith got his ideas for the 'accoutrements', as he would call them. There was an organization in Glasgow as early as 1865 which began in a dingy, deserted, singing-saloon in the overcrowded Cowcaddens district of the city to provide a meeting place and Christian instruction for boys who began work at the age of 10 or 12 in the Iron Foundries which clanged and steamed along the banks of the Forth and Clyde Canal. It was known as the Glasgow Foundry Boys' Religious Society. Several of the early leaders were Officers in the Volunteers. They held meetings on Sunday afternoons for Christian instruction and classes on weekday evenings to teach the boys to read and write. Those were the days before compulsory schooling. The boys had already had a long grimy day at the foundry. They had a quick wash and a bite to eat and then sat themselves down at desks with pens and jotters for reading and spelling on Monday and Tuesday and arithmetic on Wednesday evenings.

On Thursday nights they 'fell in' for drill under the command of a drill instructor. The Foundry Boys who were for the most part barefoot and ragged, were provided with uniforms by the Society, consisting of tunic, cap and belt. There is a picture showing a smartly turned out Foundry Boy in cap, belt and haversack.

William Smith certainly knew of the Foundry Boys' Religious Society from his Volunteer friends. He must have seen the boys parading through the suburbs on a route march with a flute band at their head. But he also had his experience with the 1st Lanarkshire Rifle Volunteers to draw upon. One could not expect The Boys' Brigade to turn out in smart waisted grey tunics, leggings and light grey helmets, spiked, which gave the Volunteers their proud name 'The Greys'. But much could be done with such accoutrements as forage caps, linen haversacks and a good leather waist belt with well-polished B.B. crest on the buckle. William Smith only insisted that his Boys be clean and tidy on parade.

It was surprising to see how effective was the simple uniform of cap and belt, while the broad white straps of the

CAP, BELT AND HAVERSACK

QUIZ, Friday, April 8, 1887.

THE BOY'S BRIGADE.—A COMPANY INSPECTION.

1st Glasgow Company Brass Band

The range of uniforms worn today

haversacks gave the Company, when drawn up in line, quite
a smart and uniform appearance.

The first 'pill box' forage cap was quite plain, with no braid or chin
strap. But within a year or two it was smartened by the addition of
two rings of white braid and the number of the Company on the front.
Later still came the chin strap and a white button on top. The pill box
was, in fact, the undress uniform of the soldier of the day. Boys of
the Boys' Brigade might well fancy themselves in the Brigade of
Guards as they formed up on parade, all caps at the same jaunty
angle.

The haversack was large enough to carry 'a modest ration' for
expeditions or sports or field manoeuvres, as many early photographs
of the B.B. show. No doubt a 'ration' carried by a hungry Boy could
mean quite a bulging bag of food. A memo from those early days
says:

> 'A plentiful supply of drinking water should, if practical, be
> provided for the Boys, but in any case they should be
> instructed to include a bottle of milk or water in the rations
> which they carry in their haversacks.'

Later the haversack was worn neatly folded and became purely
decorative.

The first leaders set themselves against a complete promotion of
exalted military-sounding ranks. Captain and Lieutenant have always
been the only two commissioned ranks of the B.B. Officer. Officers
began with dark suits and bowler hats, the daily wear of the
well-dressed city business man which many of them were. They soon
adopted the beribboned glengarry with the B.B. badge, the dark suit,
stiff white collar, black tie, tan gloves and short brown military
cane.

That is a picture of The Boys Brigade on parade as many people
still remember them. In recent years there have been a number of
changes to fit modern times. Even among the military the pill box
vanished under the influence of two world wars. The up-to-date B.B.
Boy wears a 'Field Service' cap of blue terylene and cotton with B.B.
badge set on a red surround for Company Section and a blue surround
for the Senior Section. There are many variations in accoutrements
for promoted posts such as Sergeant, Staff Sergeant, Lance Corporal
and Corporal – not to mention the Colour Sergeant and the full glory
of a kilted B.B. pipe band led by a Drum Major. And he would be
a skilled observer indeed who could instantly recognize and name the

badges for service, knowledge, skills and proficiency with which the Boys may bedeck the saluting arm. When not in uniform you should always be able to tell a B.B. Boy or Officer by his buttonhole badge – the anchor crest and Sure and Stedfast motto.

William Smith took very great care before any Boy was promoted to the rank of non-commissioned officer. A likely candidate had to promise:

1. To keep the rules of the Company, and to give regular and punctual attendance.
2. To perform faithfully and cheerfully all the duties that would be required of you in whatever rank you may be placed.
3. To endeavour at all times to set a good example to the Boys of your squad and to assist your Officers in the work of the Company.

William Smith added firmly: 'Please let me have an answer in writing . . .'

For the 1st Glasgow Company Boys of the second session there was a membership card with clear Company rules:

1. Members must give prompt and cheerful obedience to all the orders of their Officers and Non-Commissioned Officers.
2. Members must at all times set an example of good conduct to their comrades and other boys.
3. At the Bible Class there must be quietness and attention and perfect reverence during prayer.
4. Members must appear on parade looking smart and clean.
5. During drill no talking in the ranks shall be allowed except when 'standing easy'.
6. Members must always salute their Officers when they meet them or go up to address them, either on or off parade.
7. Any member who misses two drills running without good and satisfactory reason shall be struck off the roll.
8. Any member changing his address must at once intimate the change in *writing* to the Captain of the Company.
9. The penalty for breaking a Company rule shall be a mark against the Boy's name in the Company black book, and

such marks shall count more than anything else against a Boy's promotion.

Perhaps the secret of the phenomenal success of The Boys' Brigade in its early days was that Officers and Boys took 'Drill and Discipline' seriously. 'Half-heartedness is no use,' said William Smith.

The membership card of the 1st Glasgow was not all about drill and discipline and rules for good behaviour. There was promise of a swimming club, a cricket club, gymnastics with dumbbells and Indian clubs, and an ambulance class. It was all very like a junior edition of the Volunteers. A most unusual thing for boys at that time was a cheerful Club Room, comfortably furnished, with a supply of games, newspapers, magazines and writing materials, and a small library. Members of the Company were welcome there on their spare evenings to sit and talk or read or amuse themselves in their own way. Blackie, the well known publishers, were generous year by year in the supply of popular books for boys. The best known writers of the day for boys were G.A. Henty and R.M. Ballantyne. The former was represented by such titles as:

> *In Freedom's Cause: a story of Wallace and Bruce, Facing Death: A Tale of the Coal Mines*, and *Captain Bagley's Heir: A Tale of the Gold Fields of California.*

One of R. M. Ballantyne's stirring tales on the Club Room shelves was an adventure yarn called *Blown to Bits*, and his *Martin Rattler* and *Coral Island* were great favourites.

A 'treat' for the Boys was a Saturday evening visit to the Captain's new home for tea and cream cakes. William Smith married Amelia Pearson Sutherland in March 1884 and he and his 'Pearcie', as he always called her, came to live at 4 Ann Street, Hillhead, in the fashionable West End of the city, near the University and within easy walking distance of the North Woodside Mission Hall. Every Saturday evening during the winter months a Squad of twelve Boys from the Company sat down to tea in their dining-room. Mrs Smith entertained them with folk-songs in Spanish, a language she had learned in her childhood days in Gibraltar. She brought out her best silver and table linen for her tea-parties and there was always a big iced cake with the Squad number embossed in cherries. Although Smith was to travel tirelessly the length and breadth of the land to promote The Boys' Brigade, his home was always in Hillhead. It was there his two sons were born, George Stanley Smith and Douglas Pearson Smith. They were never B. B. Boys themselves, but both were to give notable service to the Movement.

In his first plans William Smith had said to his friends: 'This is going to be a great thing; let us put it into God's hands'. Now he could look to an exciting future for the Brigade – a regional, even national, perhaps an international movement. There were already several other Companies in the West End of Glasgow, led by fellow officers of the

THE LITTLE RED BOOK

1st Lanarkshire Volunteers. They met at the Smiths' home on 26th January 1885 to form themselves into a Council of the Boys' Brigade, with a Constitution which set out the rules. By the time of the first annual meeting of the Council in October, there were twelve Companies in Glasgow and three in Edinburgh. A prominent Glasgow tobacco merchant, J. Carfrae Alston, who was also a major in the 1st Lanarkshire Volunteers, was elected first President of the Council. One wonders if the Captain of the 1st Glasgow dared to remind him of the strict rule for his Boys 'not to smoke or chew tobacco'!

1ˢᵗ Glasgow Company, Boys Brigade in the Grounds of Garscube, 9ᵗʰ April, 1885

Capt. Wᵐ A. Smith. Sergt. Wᵐ H. Wylie. Sergt. John R. Jawie. Lieut. J. R. Hill. Lieut. J. B. Hill.

Fraser, Wright, Junna, W. Davidson, A. Smith, Thomson, Whitecross, Kinnoy, Bandmaster Traughton, L. Corpl. W. Stewart, Collins, Watson, Drinnan, McKenzie, Gillie, W. H. Smith, A. Sulton.
J. J. Maher, L. Corpl. Hamilton, Johnstone, Sussie, Munro, Mitchell, J. Nelson, Murray, McPhee, Carson, Aitken, McFarlane, Munn, Lymburn, Baird, W. G. Nelson, Hay, D. Davidson.
Corpl. Jannand, Hunter, Inglis, McLeod, Wilson, Junor, McLean, McPherson, Jas. Walker, McCulloch, Graham, Peddie, L. Corpl. Hendry, Cochrane, Geo. Stewart, Urquhart, Randell, L. Corpl. Dowie.

B.B. Boys from Newport with their dragon in 1980

Smith himself, though he was the founder of the Brigade, chose to undertake the duties of Secretary. All his life he had an unerring eye for men of influence in public life who could help the B.B. – city merchants, university professors, eminent churchmen and, of course, the military heroes of the day. Two stalwarts of the early days were Professor George Adam Smith, later Principal of the University of Aberdeen, and Professor Henry Drummond of the department of Natural Science at the Free Church College in Glasgow.

It was soon time to speak of the movement not only in terms of companies but also Battalions and The Brigade. The three pioneer English Companies were the 1st London, the 1st Manchester and the 1st Armitage Bridge, all enrolled on 23rd November 1885. The 1st

Newport was the pioneer in Wales in 1887 and a year later William McVicker visited Glasgow to learn all he could about the B.B., and returned to Ireland to found the 1st Belfast Company. Soon one could speak of the B.B. from Wick to the Channel Islands, and there was already a Company in the United States, to be followed by others in Canada, Auckland in New Zealand, Cape Town in South Africa, and in the West Indies. The enthusiastic Professor Henry Drummond went off on a visit to Australia, taking with him specimens of the B.B. cap, belt and haversack, and a large supply of Brigade literature which he hoped to use 'for the purpose of creating an interest in the movement throughout the Australian Colonies.'

The organization of the Brigade was now a full-time job. At the end of 1887 William Smith gave up his post in the business world and on 1st January 1888 he was at his desk as Secretary of The Boys' Brigade in their first Headquarters at 68 Bath Street, Glasgow. He was to remain Secretary, and Captain of the 1st Glasgow, and an Officer of the Volunteers, until the day of his death.

The Annual Drill Inspection for Glasgow in 1889 was held on the Spring Holiday, with 81 Companies on display and 3649 boys of all ranks, led by fife and drum and brass bands. A detachment of two NCOs and twenty men of the 15th Hussars (the King's), splendidly mounted and equipped, kept the grounds and controlled the admiring crowds.

The Founder and Secretary turned his mind to supply a guide to the origin and object and working of a Company of The Boys' Brigade. The Manual: *How to Form and Conduct a Company*, was the first of many editions to be consulted, memorized, even argued about by every generation of B.B. Officers. From the first it was known as 'the little red book'.

William Smith's daily work for many years consisted of writing long, careful letters by hand in reply to the many calls for advice and help that came in from all the new Companies, as well as dealing with enrolments, registration, subscriptions, and a hundred and one other details of administration. He also founded and edited *The Boys' Brigade Gazette*, and wrote a good deal of it himself in the early days to give good counsel for the day to day running of an ordinary Company. He has many wise, good-humoured comments to share with new Officers. About the running of a Bible class, for instance:

> Either a well-conducted Bible Class, or an address of a
> religious character to be given at the ordinary drill meeting
> ... diligence should be given to have the address short and
> full of meaning.

Make the Service bright and Boylike . . .

Warn your speakers to keep to their time. Always stop before the interest of the Boys is exhausted . . . Don't preach at the Boys.

Don't confine your selection to 'Onward, Christian soldiers!'.

Never make Boys sing what they don't believe, e.g. 'Earth is a desert drear'.

Never hedge at difficulties in the Word. Boys mix freely among sceptics.

Don't find fault with the attendance *at* the Bible Class. The Boys who are present are not the defaulters!

One question bothered William Smith even in the early days with the 1st Glasgow: 'How do we keep in touch with our Boys during the summer months?'

His military service provided him with a ready answer: CAMP. The idea of camping for Boys was a stroke of genius on Smith's part, though parents and friends must have thought him crazy. Camp was all very well for soldiers on manoeuvres or in the field of battle in faraway foreign lands. The idea that anyone should camp for fun seemed absurd, and with a crowd of mischievous boys at that! Anyway, it would certainly rain for a week – it always did during the Glasgow Fair.

The Fair Holiday in July was the time when all heavy industry in the city came to a standstill. It was the only possible time for Camp, the one brief holiday in the year many of the boys had. Few of them had ever been away from the city streets before. The Captain announced at the beginning of the winter session that the 1st Glasgow Company Camp would be held for one glorious week from Friday 16th July 1886. The cost, to be saved for at threepence a week, would be nine shillings a Boy. And, of course, prompt, regular attendance and good behaviour on drill nights and at Bible class would be essential to ensure that a Boy was fit to go to Camp.

The parents were far from sure. Their offspring would catch their death of cold, get sunstroke, fall off the boat, be bitten by a sheep or gored to death by a bull. 'Camp!' said one mother indignantly, 'My children have always had a roof over their heads, and as long as I live always will!'

The early summer days were a fever of excitement for the Boys and a masterpiece of careful organization by the Captain. We still have his notes, which were later to be used by many other would-be campers. As usual with important B.B. matters, capital letters mark the special items: Camp, Stove, Boats.

> Dishes, knives, forks, spoons should be provided in suffi-
> cient quantity for all possible requirements, including a good
> margin for kitchen and store purposes. In determining the
> quantity for each Boy, it should not be forgotten that one of
> the influences to be used in Camp is refinement.

It was a rule that in a Company Camp the Officers should mess with the Boys, 'as this ensures that the fare will be good, and has an excellent moral effect.'

Everything was to be kept spic and span. Boot brushes and blacking, soap and brooms went down on the list, as did cooking

SUMMER CAMP

*1st Leytonstone (Essex) Company
leave for camp at 4 a.m. in June 1904*

utensils, a stove, tea and coffee urns, all to be ordered in good time from a respectable ironmonger or stove-maker.

Each Boy will, of course, bring his own Bible and hymnal, and unless in cases where it would leave the family with none, he will bring a blanket also. For his own health and comfort he should further be required to bring towels, extra socks, spare cap, brush or comb, and a change of clothes if he possesses such.

Straw – 10 to 12lbs. per Boy can easily be got for a few shillings from the farmer on whose ground the Camp is, on the understanding that it is to be returned when leaving.

There is one person whom we have not yet mentioned, but without whom the Camp could not be carried on, and that is the cook. [No capital letter for him!] If a good, steady, army cook is available, he is the best man for your purpose; he will be accustomed to the manner of life and the rough and ready appliances at his command. Half-a-crown a day and his food is the proper remuneration for such a man, with the bonus of any stores left over, if he proves obliging. A fire-place is easily rigged up with the few bricks, or may be made in the ground in true military fashion.

30

1st Leytonstone Company at their first camp, Bognor 1904

Camp duties

William Smith knew well that a Boy in Camp was likely to be a hungry boy:

> Simply-cooked, plain, easily digested food is best. Any food likely to produce general stomach disorder should be avoided. The meals should be regular, and should not be stinted. There is one absolute rule for a B.B. Camp: Porridge should always form part of one's daily meal.

The general routine for the day was:

6 a.m.	Reveille.
7 a.m.	Bathing Parade (Boats) and Service of Biscuits.
9 a.m.	First Breakfast Bugle.
9.15 a.m.	Breakfast.
9.45 a.m.	Morning Prayers.
10.45 a.m.	Dress Bugle.
11.00 a.m.	Inspection of Camp and Full-Dress Parade.
1.15 p.m.	First Dinner Bugle.
1.30 p.m.	Dinner.
5.45 p.m.	First Tea Bugle.
6.00 p.m.	Tea.
7.00 p.m.	Fishing Parade (Boats).
9.30 p.m.	Evening Prayers.
9.45 p.m.	Tattoo.
10.00 p.m.	Lights Out.

Breakfast consisted of a plateful of porridge and a large cup of fresh milk, coffee, and plenty of bread and butter. Dinner was vegetable soup, mutton (boiled in the soup) and potatoes, with more bread. Tea consisted of bread, butter, jam and biscuits. 'Jam will be found very much cheaper than butter, and more highly appreciated. A piece of cake may be added as a special treat on Sunday, and on the last night.' Finally, just before lights out, a cup of cocoa and a large biscuit.

The great morning of Friday 16th July dawned for the 1st Glasgow and the Boys mustered for Roll Call at 5 a.m. at the Mission Hall in full uniform, each with his kit-bag.

'Attention!' A pause for quick inspection. Then – 'Quick march!' and the Company set off smartly behind their baggage-waggon. Even at that hour in the morning a crowd of parents and friends and envious younger brothers and sisters waved and cheered as the band struck up 'The girl I left behind me.'

The Company marched through the streets of Glasgow to the

A potato problem in camp at Aboyne

Broomielaw to join the steamer *Columba* for Tighnabruaich in the lovely Kyles of Bute. Then a short march to Auchenlochan where the 1st Glasgow had their annual camp in the local hall for a number of years before they moved to Portavadie on Loch Fyne and went under canvas. Portavadie, of long and happy B.B. memory, is now a desolate hole in the ground where oil rigs were to have been built.

The special feature of the early camps was that boats were provided for daily trips up and down the coast, for fishing expeditions and exploring the inland waters of the Firth of Clyde. The days of simply 'messing about in boats' were yet to come. Everything was under the strictest discipline. But it was new, and it was fun. Bathing parade at 7 a.m. must have been chilly indeed, even in an Argyll July. There was always a Regatta for competition among the Squads and a day when visiting friends and relatives came 'doon the watter' to see how the Boys were getting on. Sunday, of course, was a day for full-dress parade at the Parish Church in the morning and the Free Church in the evening.

Two things make the first camps very different from today. One is that the Boys remained in uniform throughout the week, except presumably when they went swimming. Photographs show them sailing, messing together, even very much 'at ease' in the long afternoons, but always stiffly clad in dark suits, heavy shoes, and the uniform accoutrements of cap, belt and haversack. It is all very different from the free and easy T-shirt and denims of today.

The other bygone event marked the day of leaving Camp. As the Boys marched through Tighnabruaich on their way to the *Columba* the local people turned out, not only to cheer them on their way, but to present each Boy with a bouquet of flowers as they broke ranks on the pier. One wonders what the Boy of today would make of this!

Woodside was ready to greet its returning heroes, flowers and all, as they marched up from the Broomielaw to the tune of 'Home Sweet Home'. Then there were tales to tell and scars to show and plans to make for next time.

Every B.B. Boy has his memories of Camp, and the stories grow in the telling. The idea of camping for Boys spread like wildfire, and the pages of *The Boys' Brigade Gazette* are filled with accounts of glorious summer days of high adventure. So may it always be! In nothing did William Smith bring so much joy to so many as in adding Camp to the vocabulary of The Boys' Brigade.

THE OUTLAWS

The Boys' Brigade in Belfast was born in turmoil and has lived bravely in turmoil ever since. The pioneer was William McVicker, a young man who wanted to do something for the boys of a poor part of Belfast where he was secretary of a Mission Sunday School. He read about William Smith's success with the B.B. in Scotland, so he took ship to Glasgow to meet Smith himself and learn how to do it. McVicker called the Founder 'a man it did me good to shake hands with', and the two men sat late at night talking of what might be done in Ireland. When he came home again, McVicker and a few enthusiastic friends drew up plans for a Belfast Company, following the example and advice of his good friend William Smith.

It was then the trouble started. The city magistrates would not hear of it. Anyone in Belfast trying to form a religious youth movement was asking for trouble, especially if it involved drill with rifles! The authorities quoted the Whiteboys Act and told McVicker to give up his idea. The Whiteboys were a secret Irish patriotic society of earlier in the century. They wore a green ribbon and campaigned against landlords, Orangemen and authority in general. The law of the land had declared them illegal some seventeen years before. But memories are long in Ireland, and there must be no excuse for further religious trouble, especially among young people. So, no B.B., which sounded very like another outlaw society, with its drill and bands and parades.

These were fighting words to William McVicker, and he was not to be daunted. He argued and persisted day after day, taking the matter eventually as far as the Lord Lieutenant himself. At last permission was granted, and the 1st Belfast Company of The Boys' Brigade was enrolled with forty Boys on the last day of the year 1888. But there were to be no rifles! The Company was connected with St. Mary Magdalene Parish Church, with William McVicker as Captain. He was to be Captain for more than 25 years, and his son William H. McVicker was Captain after him. Together they were to do as much for the B.B. in Ireland as William Smith and his sons did for the Movement at large.

The district of Belfast where the B.B. began was very poor, with large families and much overcrowding. Clothing was a problem. McVicker and his friends had a lot of debate about putting the Boys into a plain navy blue jacket to wear as a uniform as well as the accoutrements of cap, belt and haversack. They decided it would not do to give some boys a jacket and expect others to buy it, so the idea was dropped.

Route marches for recruitment and the brave sound of a bugle band made the B.B. popular. Within three years there were thirteen Companies in Belfast, enough for a Battalion, and nine others in Ulster. William McVicker used the Glasgow pattern as a model, with drill, P.T., Bible Class, and the Boys' Room, with football and cricket for out-of-doors. The Boys' Room for games and books and magazines was the most popular feature of every Company in days when there was no cinema or T.V. and no space for a restless boy at home.

But the early years in Northern Ireland were not easy. Perhaps this was because the parents were not greatly interested, or were suspicious of a movement that had been outlawed at first by the authorities. The more prosperous Belfast citizens were cautious. They did not supply the powerful leadership which Glasgow city merchants and churchmen gave so enthusiastically and where almost every B.B. Captain was also an Officer in the Volunteers. Many Companies in Northern Ireland did not survive, and were disbanded. 'Drill is rather a weak point with us,' McVicker had to confess. Only three Companies in Belfast have an unbroken record since 1890.

Nevertheless, there was courage and a good spirit. One harmonious feature was that the Irish Companies were widely interdenominational, representing the Church of Ireland and the Presbyterian, Baptist, Methodist, and Moravian Churches. The Officers knew that their first loyalty was to 'The advancement of Christ's Kingdom among Boys'. Field Days, Battalion competitions and Camp all fostered *esprit de corps*, and the Annual Inspections made a brave display. It was a proud day when the Battalion was reviewed by Field-Marshal Baron Roberts, V.C., of Kandahar and Waterford, Commander-in-Chief in Ireland and the supreme hero of the British Empire.

William Smith came frequently to Northern Ireland to see how this lively offspring was getting on. There was an Irish happy-go-lucky attitude in some Companies which did not always accord with the Founder's strict standards. For instance, it was minuted by the Belfast Battalion Executive in 1910:

> The Commanding Officer of the Battalion is hereby given
> power to summon any Companies he thinks fit to a
> preliminary drill and, if necessary, to order any incompetent
> Company not to parade at the Battalion Inspection.

A young Dublin clergyman came to Belfast in 1891 to visit a friend. He came across 'the little red book' on the study table in his host's house, and sat down to read the B.B. Manual from end to end. He went south full of excitement, and the 1st Dublin Company was the result. It was the beginning of one of the truly excellent Battalions of The Boys' Brigade.

The years of World War I were difficult for the Belfast Battalion, first because of an epidemic of scarlet fever which closed down church halls, and later when the military authorities decreed that every Company which used drill in its programme must have a permit to do so. In the political disturbances of the early twenties there was danger at every street corner and a curfew which ordered everyone indoors by 10 p.m.

But there were flashes of sunshine in the general gloom. The Battalion bought a twelve acre farm at Ganaway in County Down, and that was to bring golden memories of Camp to one generation of Boys after another. And Belfast proudly sent a thousand Officers and Boys to the Jubilee Review at Hampden Park, Glasgow, in 1933, by way of Larne and Stranraer at an inclusive cost of ten shillings and sixpence a head.

In World War II Belfast was right in the firing line. In the Spring of 1941 enemy bombers dropped incendiaries, high explosive bombs and parachute bombs all across the city, damaging or destroying the dock area, churches, hospitals and the work-places and homes of ordinary people. For many weeks on end, ten thousand men, women and children used to trudge out of the city every night to seek shelter in barns, under haystacks, even in drains in the surrounding countryside. Everyday B.B. activities were continually interrupted and rationing of food, petrol and clothing made daily life dreary.

The seventies brought political unrest again, and the end of that is not even in sight. It is dangerous to go out at night and several members of the B.B. have died or suffered grievously from gunshot wounds. Bursts of gunfire bring sleepless nights, the city sky red with the glow of raging fires. There are rows upon rows of derelict buildings and rubble. Brigade House has been set on fire, repaired and redecorated, and set on fire again. It is hard indeed to be 'Sure and Stedfast' in endless days and nights of violence and civil unrest. But the Boys' Brigade in Belfast stands fast. Blow, bugles, blow!

Belfast Boy handing out 'First for Boys' leaflets in the shopping centre

Almost from the beginning The Boys' Brigade had its critics, and they had plenty to say. The main attack was against the B.B.'s military look. The Founder's own words were: 'The Boys' Brigade is a religious movement, using military methods'. William Smith wanted to use 'Drill and Discipline' to produce some order in an unruly Sunday School. He believed that lively boys would enjoy the novelty of wearing uniform and the discipline of obeying orders smartly. The Volunteers were his model, and the B.B. was organized quite openly with the military pattern of Privates, NCOs and Officers, drilled in Squads, Companies, Battalions, not to speak of Colours, the Band, Camp, and an Annual Inspection or Review under the eye of a Field Marshal.

William Smith thought he had nothing to apologize for. He knew what he was doing. 'The Boys' Brigade does not concern itself about recruiting for Her Majesty's Services, but it holds that, were all our forces largely leavened by men of the types aimed at in the training of the Boys, this country would be indebted to The Brigade.'

It was the rifles which caused the deepest offence. William Smith's training was with the 1st Lanarkshire *Rifle* Volunteers, and the rifle was as important as a soldier's right hand. Indeed, it was part of the training of the Volunteers that they never went to bed at night without their rifles and uniforms ready for instant use at the call of duty. It seemed only natural in those days that the only good drill was one that included the precise thud and slap and smart control of rifles exercised in precision. Some of the earliest manuals available from B.B. Headquarters were:

> *Infantry Drill: as revised by Her Majesty's Command.* Price one shilling. *Manual Exercises for the Rifle and Carbine.* 3d post paid, and *Firing Exercises.* Threepence.

There was also a note in *The Boys' Brigade Gazette* to say that the Regulation Rifle approved by the Executive of the B.B. was now available at a reduced price of four shillings each.

The rifles, of course, were dummies, for training purposes only. But some of the churches, the religious newspapers, and the members of the Peace Society swung into attack on the B.B. Peacelovers they might claim to be, but they did not mince their words. The religious papers cried out that the Boys of the B.B. had caught 'the dangerous fever', all thirsting to be soldiers in the Army or Militia. A speaker in Liverpool claimed that the Boys were full of the spirit of jingoism, ready 'to blaze up like matchwood and plunge us into desperate

THE PRAYING AND FIGHTING MONSTER

strife'. Others said that the B.B. was a dodge of the War Office to introduce conscription.

The Secretary of the Peace Society had a rush of words to the head in a letter he sent out to newspapers all over Britain:

> I am of the opinion that this new-born Scottish monster, which claims God and the Devil for parents, will require unceasing watchfulness on the part of friends of peace generally. It is unquestionably the master-stroke of Mars, by which ministers of Christ's Gospel are used as recruiting sergeants for the British Army.

He urged a crusade against The Brigade, in season and out of season, to crush this 'young praying and fighting monster.'

Many worthy church people were horrified at the idea of boys playing at soldiers in mission halls up and down the land. But William Smith was not to be daunted. Certainly he believed in drill and discipline, he declared, but the aim of the B.B. was to subdue and temper the warlike spirit, not to encourage it. He held to drilling and marching as the finest way of teaching Obedience, Order, Reverence and Self-Respect, and the rifle was a traditional part of drill. So William Smith went up and down the country, speaking at every annual meeting of The Brigade in all the major cities, defending the Object and method of The Boys' Brigade, pointing to the manly appearance of the boys, appealing to the pride of their parents and the good feeling of the citizens at large. He knew that he had on his side a goodly array of Honorary Vice-Presidents – Field-Marshal Viscount Wolseley, Commander in Chief of Her Majesty's Forces, Field-Marshal Earl Roberts of Kandahar, heroes both to old and young, G.A. Henty, whose thrilling adventure tales were devoured by every healthy British boy, and Archbishops, Bishops, Moderators in plenty to support and applaud the ideals of The Boys' Brigade. Against such an establishment the voices of do-gooders were thin and shrill.

The rifle was not compulsory, but most Companies were equipped with them, as many of the early photographs show. The Enfield Companies came to be famous for their display of bayonet exercises. But there were places where rifles were not used, Belfast, for example, where even a dummy weapon was too warlike a symbol for that troubled part of the United Kingdom. Dublin Battalion also tactfully decided to drill without rifles.

When The Boys' Brigade began in Plymouth there was a special resolution precluding the use of rifles because the 2nd Plymouth Company was connected with The Society of Friends.

William Smith was satisfied that in military organization and drill he could create a movement which had real attraction for boys, and foster an *esprit de corps* which would hold their loyalty. By and large the nation backed him, though there was always a murmur of criticism about the rifles until eventually they were abandoned after World War I. The basic Aim and Object of The Boys' Brigade, except for one word, has remained unaltered since the founding of the first Company in 1883.

First officers and N.C.O.'s 1st Glasgow Company 1885

Turn of The Century

Queen Victoria's Empire reached its zenith in 1897, the year of the Diamond Jubilee of her reign. June 22nd was a day to be remembered and spoken of to children's children, when the Queen Empress rode in an open carriage drawn by six white horses through the streets of London to celebrate sixty glorious years at an open-air thanksgiving service on the steps of St. Paul's Cathedral.

The sun shone all through the day, and the city was a pageant of the widest Empire the world had ever known. In the royal procession there were representatives of the dominions and colonies far across the seas – Indian rajahs, African chiefs, officers and men from service forces in Borneo, Hong Kong, West Africa and Jamaica – and stiffly-clad princes and statesmen to pay their respects from the foreign powers of half the world. The Queen's carriage was thronged by cavalry jingling in their scarlet and buff and blue and grey tunics, gleaming accoutrements and plumed helmets. Fifty thousand troops marched through London that day in the full dress uniform of their regiments, from the famed fighting men of the North West Frontier of India to the stalwart kilted Highlanders of Scotland. The Union Jack fluttered from every window and rooftop and the citizens of London cheered themselves hoarse as the bands thumped out 'Soldiers of the Queen.'

The Boys' Brigade had reason to share proudly in the pageantry, and they did. The returns for the very first session in Glasgow which had ended only thirteen years before on 30th April 1884 had declared: 1 Company, 3 Officers, 30 Boys. Now the Brigade commemorated the royal occasion with 'a loyal and dutiful address' in the name of 790 Companies, 2900 Officers and 35,000 Boys, a tribute of esteem, loyalty and appreciation. Besides this they could claim 27,000 Boys in the United States of America, 4000 in Canada, 2000 in South Africa, as well as Companies in the West Indies, Australia, New Zealand and India. The Boys' Brigade was not merely of the Empire. It was a truly international movement.

The Brigade could count the Diamond Jubilee Year an important stage in their own story. In recent years Brigade Council had met and been publicly recognized in many of the major cities of the United Kingdom – Sheffield, Bristol, Liverpool, Plymouth, Belfast, Carlisle, Dublin, Edinburgh, as well as in its native Glasgow. In this special year of rejoicing, the Annual Meeting was planned for London, the Metropolis of Empire as the B.B. *Gazette* reminded its readers, where, by happy coincidence, a B.B. Captain was Lord Mayor.

The London Boys and visitors who saw the royal pageant could remind themselves that the Queen had acknowledged their parade

lines drawn up in her honour in half a dozen cities of her kingdom. Boys of the London Battalion were invited by the authorities to be present at a special performance of the Royal Military Tournament in commemoration of the Longest Reign.

Queen Victoria drives to the Diamond Jubilee Thanksgiving Service at St. Paul's

The favourite stories of Henty and Kipling seemed to come alive before the very eyes of the Boys who watched and cheered. There passed before them on their nodding chargers the heroes of Empire who were their own B.B. Vice-Presidents: Earl Wolseley, Commander in Chief of the British Army, who had been a soldier and wounded before the age of twenty, long before the Indian Mutiny, the Ashanti and Zulu Wars, and Tel-el-Kebir. Any full-blooded boy could recite his campaigns. And Field-Marshal Lord Roberts of Kandahar, V.C., on the very Arab steed which he had ridden at the head of his troops on his victorious Afghan expedition. It was the kindly and much-loved 'Bobs' who was to ask his Royal Highness, the Duke of Cornwall and York (the future King George V) if he would graciously become the first Royal Patron of The Boys' Brigade.

41

It was indeed a year of 'dominion over palm and pine'. It led William Smith to affirm openly that there was no reason to apologize for the military features of The Boys' Brigade. Drill and discipline, he declared again, were the secret of their *esprit de corps*. No wonder the Boys' favourite hymns at Battalion Display or Company Bible Class were: 'Onward Christian Soldiers!' and 'Fight the good fight!'

The turn of the century saw The Boys' Brigade in very good heart. There was a buoyant increase of a record 6000 Boys caused in part by the unrest and excitement of the South African War. There was a military air throughout the country, with much argument for and against, and few Boys did not have a relative in the Regulars, Reserves, Militia or Volunteers. Not only Princes and Field-Marshals, Archbishops and Lord Mayors, but also the widespread goodwill of the churches supported the B.B. in its Aim and Object. The attack from the religious press on bloodthirsty ruffians had largely died under the tidal wave of patriotism and loyalty.

The move to the Albert Hall for the Annual London Meeting and Demonstration was an important step. The Earl of Aberdeen, Honorary President and life-long friend of The Boys' Brigade, was to preside. There were to be more than 2000 Boys in uniform with a programme of displays which included:

Ambulance Work by the North London Battalion
Gymnastics by the West London Battalion
Physical Drill by the City and East London Battalion
Dumb-Bell Exercises by the West Kent Battalion
Bayonet Exercises by the United Enfield Companies
Company Drill by the South London Battalion
Battalion Drill and Trooping the Colours by the
united London Battalions

A Brass Band and the Bugle Band of the 1st Enfield Company was to play during the evening. And to crown all, a Pipe Band of Scottish Boys from the 102nd Glasgow Company was to raise the roof with the brave skirl of the pipes. A lady well-wisher in Govan was paying the pipers' fare to London and all their expenses for a sight-seeing tour.

In the midst of all this heady excitement, the Boy was, as always, the Boy. A Private who aspired to promotion set down his painstaking answer to drill notes in the Company examination: The improved method of forming fours is as follows: Take a pace to the left with your right foot, and a pace to the right with your left foot.

A Brigade President, Lord Guthrie, once said: When anybody asked me how they could get an idea of what The Boys' Brigade stood for, I used to say: 'Read our motto, and then go and take a good look at Sir William Smith, our Founder and our Brigade Secretary'.

From the day he started the 1st Glasgow, William Smith was Captain of his original Company, on parade, at Bible Class, and at summer Camp. He gave of his best, and he expected the best. He could warmly commend a Boy, an Officer, a Company for work well done, but he was not given to lavish praise. Duty was duty, and it was its own reward.

THE MAN WHO SPELT 'BOY'

Sir William Alexander Smith

The Founder was very much a man of commonsense. He had little time, for instance, for Boys singing hymns which were ludicrously unreal to them. Lead, kindly Light was a fine hymn, but surely not for the B.B.? How could he associate the Boys as he knew them with ecstatic hailing of angel faces which they had loved long since and lost awhile? 'A Boy who sticks a pin into another Boy gives promise of being a finer man than he who sings demurely, "I want to be an angel".' Nor was Smith happy with zealous Officers who thought of Camp as a special opportunity to work on the Boys' feelings and convert them to a particular brand of religion. Camp was for health and enjoyment. Officers should do their work thoroughly, earnestly and devotedly, and leave the issue in God's hands. He insisted that Officers and Boys should share in all the adventure, weather, sports, hardships and fun of Camp, and that they must be together at meals. 'If a dinner does not turn out a culinary success, Officers should not immediately dine at the nearest hotel.'

Rules are rules, and in the B.B. they are made after careful discussion and often a plebiscite of the whole Movement. So The Brigade must be loyal to them:

> We heard the other day of a B.B. Officer wearing an imitation of a military uniform, and of another Officer who so far forgot what was due to his military rank in the Volunteers as to wear his Volunteer Officer's uniform in Camp with his Boys. How can Officers expect Boys to keep Company rules if they themselves fail to keep Brigade rules?

Lieutenant-Colonel Smith of the 1st Lanark Rifle Volunteers was as sensitive to the regard of his military fellow-officers as was Captain Smith for the good name of The Boys' Brigade.

As Brigade Secretary, William Smith kept an eye on everything concerning the B.B. up and down the world, and his daily correspondence tray showed it. He had a sharp eye for any slovenliness or a breach of regulations. Every Battalion Report was read, noted, and remembered. Liverpool's Report was a model of lucidity and order, and they were particularly good at Ambulance work. Ayr Battalion was commended for its splendid annual flower show. Summer Camp is the feature in which Manchester excels all other Battalions. There was a most successful Bible Class in Hull to be noted, and West Kent was progressing excellently. 1st Newport sent him a photograph of the Company in all the glory of their Camp sun-hats, which the Secretary enjoyed and printed in the *Gazette*. But he reminded them that sun-hats are sanctioned only for Camp and are on no account to take the place of the regulation uniform cap for parade purposes.

But what was going on in Nottingham? 'Who ever heard of the ranks of Colonel or Major in The Boys' Brigade? Yet these appear on the first page of the Nottingham Battalion Report. Not good enough!' At the same time, remember that it was Nottingham which produced the splendid B.B. hymn, 'Underneath the Banner of The Boys' Brigade'.

Edinburgh had two irregularities to be noted in the way of accoutrements: red edging on NCOs' stripes, and special Band caps. Cardiff had five Vice-Presidents and Carlisle had six, while the Brigade Constitution provided for only one. 'Study the Manual,' wrote William Smith, 'and obey the Rules!'

He went to see for himself, tirelessly, up and down the country. In the year of the semi-jubilee of The Brigade William Smith made extensive visits to Companies in Orkney and Shetland in the far north and a few months later inspected the Jersey Companies in the south. That same session he was also in Bristol, South Wales, Cork, Leeds, Melrose, Newcastle-on-Tyne and London. Everywhere he was received with enthusiasm by the Boys.

He paid a visit to America at the cordial invitation of General H.P. Bope who was Commander-in-Chief of the United Boys' Brigades of America and he saw B.B. work in New York, Boston, Philadelphia, Washington, Baltimore, Pittsburgh, Cleveland, Chicago and St. Louis. He met the President of the United States, Theodore Roosevelt, who thanked him for all he had done for Boys throughout the world. Smith found 'the American Boy a very charming product of civilization, well set up, keen and alert, with a fascinating frankness and brightness which are simply irresistible'. But he could not approve of the extravagant ranks and uniforms – Officers all dressed up with swords, braided tunics, peaked caps and crests. The Boys wore blue drill jackets with seven brass buttons, a black leather belt, white duck trousers, brown leggings and a French chasseur cap with cross guns in front. They were festooned with medals and decorations of every kind. He noted that age limits were not strictly kept at either end. 'Some mere children of 9 years were to be observed, while in several cases the "Boys" in the ranks were of such mature age that they were able to refer to their wives!'

The semi-jubilee of The Boys' Brigade was marked in Glasgow by the presentation of an address of appreciation and a portrait of the Founder subscribed by the citizens. It still hangs in the Art Galleries of the city. About the same time new and spacious Headquarters were opened by the Earl of Aberdeen, the Honorary President, on the fourth floor of the handsome Merchants' House of Glasgow.

In July 1909 the 1st Glasgow were, as usual, at their old camping ground at Tighnabruaich in the Kyles of Bute. On Wednesday evening Captain Smith quietly left Camp to travel overnight to London. On Thursday he visited Buckingham Palace to receive the honour of knighthood from His Majesty, King Edward VII. On Friday morning Sir William A. Smith was back in camp to receive a tumultuous welcome from the Boys.

The Albert Hall Demonstration was the highlight of the B.B. year. Sir William Smith was there as usual on Thursday 7th May, 1914, with a royal chairman, His Serene Highness, Prince Alexander of Teck, and the great building packed with Boys and parents and friends of The Brigade.

The next day Sir William was at meetings of the B.B. Executive in the London Office. All at once he took ill, and he did not regain consciousness. He died on Sunday 10th May in St. Bartholomew's Hospital, barely sixty years of age.

The whole Movement was stunned by the news. Every Officer and Boy felt that he knew the Founder. It was he who had always said: 'Put the Boy first'. Now there was mourning up and down the land. Four thousand Boys filled St. Paul's Cathedral to its furthest corners on Friday 15th May for the memorial service. In the choir stalls were leaders of all the Boys' organizations who acknowledged Sir William as their Pioneer – The Church Lads' Brigade, The London Diocesan Church Lads' Brigade, The Catholic Boys' Brigade, The Jewish Lads' Brigade, the Boys' Life Brigade, and The Boy Scouts under their chief, Sir Robert Baden-Powell. They were there to pay tribute to the Founder of the Movement which had been First for Boys.

After the service eight Staff Sergeants carried the coffin of Sir William from the chapel of St. Bartholomew's Hospital while the Guard of Honour of the 62nd London and 3rd Enfield stood with arms reversed. The Band of the 103rd London Company began to play Abide With Me as the cortege stepped slowly into the night.

At Euston station the West London Battalion provided a Guard of Honour. Perhaps the most moving moment of all came as the train sped north through the night, when a detachment of the 2nd Rugby Company sounded the Last Post from a bleak and lonely platform as a farewell to the Founder.

Glasgow has always known itself to be the home of The Boys' Brigade and the whole city went into mourning. After the funeral service in College and Kelvingrove Church a Bugler headed the march

Funeral of Sir William Smith
Glasgow May 1914

through the city, followed by two Companies of Glasgow Sergeants and massed Brass and Pipe Bands. The 1st Glasgow Company had the place of honour preceding the funeral coach with its four horses and postillions. Behind them came a great company of mourners from The Brigade of Great Britain and Ireland and past and present members of Sir William Smith's regiment. Several of the original members of the 1st Glasgow were there. The three miles to the place of burial were lined by 7000 Boys of the Glasgow Battalion and behind them thousands of men, women and children who had come to pay tribute to the man the whole city knew. They remembered his soldierly bearing, the set of his head, his alert and steady eye, the firm grip of his hand. He was without doubt a Christian gentleman.

47

Sir William Smith was buried in the Western Necropolis, and the last act of the day was when the Boys of the 1st Glasgow filed past the open grave and each cast into it a white flower. Then they sang the B.B. hymn 'Onward, Christian Soldiers!', and the solitary bugler sounded 'The Last Post.'

Memorial services for Sir William Smith were held in every city of the United Kingdom where the B.B. was known. Those who were present were never to forget that solemn day. But all who knew Sir William Smith were quick to resolve that the B.B. should go from strength to strength. That was the best tribute they could pay to their beloved Founder. That resolve was best summed up in the words of the telegram from the King: 'Sir William Smith's name will ever be remembered as the Founder and friend of The Boys' Brigade.'

From that day to this the story of William A. Smith has been told from one generation of B.B. Boys to another, and Founder's Day has been kept on the last Sunday in October each year to commemorate his birth and life.

'It was left to Sir William,' said Lord Guthrie, 'to spell the word Boy with a capital "B".'

World War I broke on the Western world on August 4th 1914, and things were never the same again.

There was an immediate loyal flocking to the Colours. All over the country Officers of The Boys' Brigade, many of whom were already in the Reserves or Territorials, went off to their military or naval units. Stanley Smith, for example, son of the Founder and now Assistant Brigade Secretary, was called up to his regiment, the 5th Scottish Rifles, at the beginning of August and went almost immediately to Flanders. His brother Douglas came in to Headquarters to take his place until he himself was called up to the Navy.

Soon the B.B. *Gazette* was to record page after page of B.B. men on active service. The first total in February 1915 showed almost 10,000 names. The second list, only a month later, doubled that figure. Then came the sad lists of men killed in action, or missing, believed killed, and the record of bravely-won decorations. Some 400,000 Old Boys and Officers served in World War I, and among them eleven were awarded the Victoria Cross for the highest gallantry.

Every regiment in the kingdom, Regular or Territorial, had its quota of B.B. Old Boys. Perhaps the most famous in B.B. annals was the 16th Service Battalion of The Highland Light Infantry, recruited entirely by the Glasgow Battalion of the Brigade for 'Kitchener's Army'. The 16th was to distinguish itself in some of the bloodiest battles of four long years of war – the Somme, Beaumont Hamel, Passchendaele and Arras.

Here are some brief B.B. glimpses of those faraway, heroic, tragic days:

An early episode was the seige of Antwerp in the north of Belgium by the German Army. British Naval Brigades were sent to the relief and evacuation of the city.

> Among the men was Murray Macdougal, a Bugler Boy of fourteen, a member of The Boys' Brigade. He had certainly no business to be there, but in the haste of sudden embarkation he had joined the troops and was not noticed until Belgium was reached. During the thirty-two miles march which followed the evacuation of the city he stuck it with the best.

One outcome of the devastation of Belgium was that thousands of Belgian refugees, men, women and children, flocked across the Channel. The B.B. pledged itself to be guardian to some of the desolate and bewildered children who sought sanctuary in Britain.

ARMAGEDDON AND AFTER

The youngsters arrived, duly labelled, at Charing Cross Station, to be made much of by their new B.B. friends. It was a gleam of compassion in a dark time of war, and the young Belgians never forgot their welcome. Some of them stayed to make their homes here.

Some vivid 'Scraps from an Officer's Diary' came from the pen of Captain F.W. Stevens of the 1st Essex Regiment, who was a Captain of the Boys' Brigade:

> Once again in the front line, 'somewhere in France'. The dull brown earth is tinged with green; flowers are fraternizing with wire entanglements; the trill of a lark in the clear blue sky mingles with the distant drone of an aeroplane; the laughter of children in the nearby ruined village alternates with an intermittent scream of an enemy shell; a plough is moving slowly across land within range of the guns.

From the Senior Service there came the story of Boy William Walker. He was 16 years of age and a former member of the 4th London Company of The Boys' Brigade. William Walker became adept at bugling, and that stood him in good stead when he joined the Royal Navy. He became bugler aboard H.M.S. *Calliope* when she led her squadron into the turmoil of the Battle of Jutland on 31st May 1916. 'Young Bill', as he was known, had to stand on the bridge with the Captain and sound the order 'Commence'. Thereafter he stood by his Captain through the fury of the fiercest naval battle of the war. *Calliope* was hit five times in her pursuit of the enemy destroyers. Late in the day a splinter of a shell struck Boy Walker, wounding him severely in the side. He stood at his post until he fainted from loss of blood. Later, in hospital, he was visited by His Majesty King George V and, greatest honour of all, he was given a specially inscribed bugle by the Admiral of the Fleet himself, 'Jellicoe of Jutland', in recognition of his gallantry.

At home, the service and sacrifice of B.B. combatants told heavily on the Movement. There was an increasing shortage of Officers and Staff-Sergeants, who were now with the Forces. Lighting restrictions cut short evening drills. Summer Camps were not allowed on the coast or in areas prohibited to everyone except the Army. Many Companies were forced to give up altogether. By the final year of the war B.B. numbers were very considerably down, all over the country. It is a fine tribute to the Movement that two rest huts for the troops, one at Rouen and one in Edinburgh, were paid for, maintained and staffed by the B.B. throughout the years of war.

It was a confused and troubled time for The Boys' Brigade. There

The rest hut for the troops in Edinburgh

is no doubt, looking back, that they greatly missed the wise leadership and firm guiding hand of Sir William Smith. For example, the War Office had proposed as early as 1910 that various Brigades for boys should be recognized by the Army Council as Cadet Corps. The bribes offered were considerable – they could have the loan of Government Camp equipment, a supply of disused Army carbines, the free use of firing ranges and drill halls, and the privilege of inspection by Army Officers in uniform. The Army Council would cut short the training period for any recruit who had been in the Cadets. They would, in fact, have a constant supply of almost readymade soldiers.

The B.B. Executive called for a poll of opinion all through the Movement. The reply was emphatic: nearly 90% voted the idea to be detrimental to the primary Object of The Boys' Brigade. The churches were against it; parents disapproved; friends and supporters would have none of it. The Boys' Brigade had a commitment to the advancement of Christ's Kingdom among the Boys in its care, and the promotion of true Christian manliness. It was not their task to provide the War Office with drilled and obedient cannon fodder. William Smith firmly told Haldane so at the War Office. As a result, all the privileges the Army had to offer were at once withdrawn from The Boys' Brigade. But the B.B. could call its soul its own.

Other organizations took up the Cadet idea, and some B.B. Companies were left free to do so. In days of war the glamour of uniform and training made a very strong appeal to boys whose fathers and older brothers were fighting for King and Country.

The new and much younger movement, The Boy Scouts, won the hearts of many boys, with its healthy, open-air, adventurous image. Major-General R.S.S. Baden-Powell, the hero of Mafeking, was an Honorary Vice-President and good friend of the B.B. He had been Inspecting Officer of the Glasgow Battalion on their 21st birthday, and it was on that occasion that William Smith suggested that he might write a book for boys who were training to be good citizens. The result was an article, 'Scouting for Boys' which appeared in the B.B. *Gazette* in June 1906. B.P. wrote:

> The object of the scheme is to develop among Boys a power of sympathizing with others, a spirit of self-sacrifice and patriotism, and generally to prepare them for becoming good citizens. The method suggested is to make Boys observant of details, and to develop their reasoning powers, and at the same time to inculcate in them the spirit of self-denial and of obedience to duty.

We can see how Baden-Powell and William Smith learned from one another. There was even a time when there were B.B. Scouts, with wide-brimmed hats, knapsacks and all. 'Scouting for Boys', first written for the B.B., was the germ of an idea which grew to be the great worldwide Scout Movement, founded by B.P. some 25 years after the Brigade.

The end of the war years found The Boys' Brigade unsure of itself. There was great restlessness over the matter of uniform. A speaker at the Manchester Council meeting in 1917 could say that he admired the wonderful insight of William Smith in fixing on the simple uniform: cap, belt and haversack. But he went on: 'These Victorian days are past. Numbers are dropping, and the uniform is to blame, especially the "pill box". It is completely obsolete, and the Boys hate it.'

THE BOYS' BRIGADE

OBJECT : The Object of the Brigade is the advancement of Christ's Kingdom among Boys, and the promotion of habits of Obedience, Reverence, Discipline, Self-Respect, and all that tends towards a true Christian Manliness.

If you want to—

PLAY FOOTBALL — OR CRICKET — OR SWIM —

TO KNOW ABOUT BANDAGES — RUN A RACE — CAMP —

THEN JOIN
THE BOYS' BRIGADE

RECRUITS must be keen Boys over 12 years old, prepared to attend with unfailing regularity. The Boy who gave you this will tell you when and where to join. Fill in this Form and bring it with you.

1ST GLASGOW ....Company

Name.. Age...................

Address ....

That started it! During the next year or two some extraordinary experiments in uniform were tried out. The Executive proposed a full khaki uniform, and that gained a good deal of approval. Scottish Companies were encouraged to experiment with kilt and balmoral. There was even a special tartan approved and registered as 'The Sir

William Smith of Pennyland Tartan' for the sole use of The Boys' Brigade.

But soon complaints poured in. The tailor's dummies of the illustrations in the *Gazette* were glamorous enough, with chevrons, leggings, and rakish caps. But the real Boys were not. The proportion of younger Boys was considerable at this time and small boys and khaki did not harmonize. They looked like mascots. As for the 'alternative cap', it was known everywhere as 'the convict's cap'.

Brigade Council changed its mind again, and suggested grey or blue. Grey won the vote, and elaborate details were worked out. The tunic was to be grey, with dark blue facings and a low collar. Dark blue shoulder straps would carry the letters B.B. in brass. It was left to Officers Commanding Companies 'whether they adopt Breeches or Shorts, or both'. Puttees were to be dark blue. The cap was to be of Air Force pattern, grey with blue piping, and the badge an eight-pointed brass star. There was to be a similar uniform for Officers, but with a Service peak cap.

The new uniform brought no peace. Some complained about the top-heavy effect of a man's uniform upon a very small Boy. Others were outspoken about the orphanage or reformatory look of the grey outfit. The mixture of uniforms on a Battalion parade looked ridiculous. It was particularly remarked that the strongest and smartest Companies on parade were wearing the traditional cap, belt and haversack.

The truth was that the B.B. was looking for its image, and a mirror was the last place to find it. The wise and far-seeing H. Arnold Wilson of Milngavie reminded his fellow-officers of the move against militarism that was bound to come after the war. The Movement should stop fussing about uniform and shoulder straps and brass and puttees and be sure and stedfast to their Object.

Certainly there were many younger Boys. Some Companies were already taking in Boys under the age of 12, whatever the rules might say. Others experimented unofficially with Junior Corps. In the year 1917 two splendid B.B. men, F. C. Carey Longmore, Captain of the 1st Warley Company, and Douglas Pearson Smith, second son of the Founder, proposed a properly organized new movement for younger Boys, with its own uniform, title and training. It was to be known as 'The Boy Reserves'.

FIFTY YEARS ON

The Jubilee in 1933 was the biggest event ever held in the history of The Boys' Brigade. Numbers were at their very best, with a total enrolment of 111,871 Boys and 52,219 Life Boys. Jubilee weeks, pageants, displays and thanksgivings were to be held up and down the land.

In London the celebrations began with the traditional Royal Albert Hall Demonstration, made memorable by the parade of the Original Company and the pioneer English and Irish Companies – the 1st Glasgow, the 1st London and the 1st Belfast. On Midsummer Day the London Jubilee Review was held at Wembley in a deluge of rain. That very day the Test Match was washed out, an Air Force Pageant curtailed and a Territorial Review cancelled. But London's B.B. carried on. The huge arena at Wembley became a lake, but H.R.H. the Duke of Gloucester gallantly stood to attention throughout the downpour to review the Trooping of the Colour, the Massed Bands, and the March Past in slow time. The most impressive moment was the parade of the Old Boys, column after column, encircling the whole arena. The spectators rose as one man, and there was a continuous roar of cheers. It was a B.B. day to be remembered.

In contrast the sun shone all week on 'Glasgow 1933', the great B.B. event of the year. The whole hospitable city took the Brigade to its heart for a week of Jubilee. The railways provided cards so that Boys could save week by week for the trip. The 30th London Company bought their own second-hand bus and emblazoned their name and crest on it for the journey north. Belfast and Dublin chartered special steamers for their hundreds of Officers, Boys, parents and friends. The Dublin Old Boys went one better by chartering *The Lady Munster* to be their floating hotel at the Broomielaw in the heart of Glasgow for the whole weekend of their visit. Special trains brought uniformed Officers and Boys to Glasgow from all over Britain.

The Glasgow Companies began their own thanksgiving on Sunday 3rd September when every one of the city's 253 Companies paraded at morning service in their own church, each Company being accompanied by its Old Boys. Each night during the following week there were route-marches, open-air displays in the City's beautiful public parks, football matches, swimming galas, sports meetings and fancy-dress processions.

On the Wednesday, Colonel John A. Roxburgh, Brigade President, unveiled a bronze tablet in the 1st Glasgow's headquarters in North Woodside Road which was to be a place of pilgrimage for every B.B. visitor that week. The tablet read:

1883   1933

TO THE GLORY OF GOD

in Proud Remembrance of the First Fifty Years of

THE BOYS' BRIGADE

And with Thanksgiving for more than
One Million Boys who throughout the World have
benefited by its Training, this Tablet is erected
within the place where, under God,

WILLIAM ALEXANDER SMITH

founded the Movement on the
Fourth Day of October, 1883.

The Jubilee lapel badge was to be seen all over the city. To be a B.B. Boy that glorious week was to walk like a king. And wherever you went you heard the stirring Jubilee song, written and composed by a B.B. Officer, Thomas Henderson:

> For fifty years the work's been done,
> And now it's ours to carry on!
> Stedfast as our fathers were,
> Sure in the faith that won;
> Hear the song, clear and strong,
> Down through the ranks go ringing;
> 'For fifty years the work's been done,
> And now it's ours to carry on!'

The Jubilee Camp was at Dechmont, a few miles from the city, attended by two representative Boys from every Company in The Boys' Brigade, and from Denmark, Canada, Singapore and Nigeria. From the earliest hours of Friday 8th September, Transport Officers met a stream of Boys at the stations and docks and sent them on by rail to the Camp. There were 400 bell tents, 17 dining marquees and 2 super-marquees for canteen and concerts, as well as a fully equipped field hospital with 3 doctors and a dentist in attendance. Each Boy at Dechmont was at once allocated to a Battalion, Company, and Tent, and there was a Glasgow Boy in every tent to be host and guide and friend. No one who was there could ever forget Dechmont – the new friends, the games, the sing-songs, the canteen, Camp Prayers, the Drumhead Service, and the final lighting of the Fire of Friendship on Dechmont Hill.

On the Friday night, in the presence of thousands of Campers, six NCOs' put their names to a parchment containing a secret message of greeting and goodwill addressed to their successors, the Boys of the Centenary Year, 1983. The chosen six were:

> Sergeant Hizzey of the 1st Glasgow
> Sergeant Gray of the 39th Belfast
> Corporal Choy Ah Soo of the 2nd Singapore
> Colour-Sergeant Morrish of the 11th Cardiff
> Colour-Sergeant Martin of the 12th Brighton
> Sergeant Urquhart of the 214th Glasgow.

Thus they represented the Original Company, Ireland, Overseas, Wales, England and Scotland.

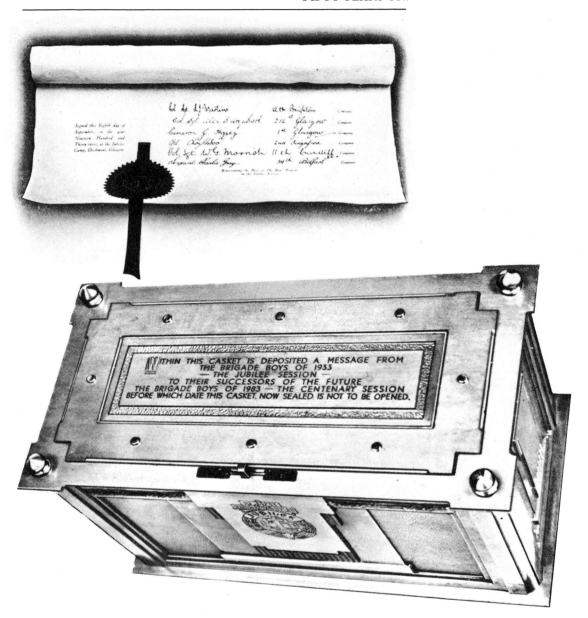

The parchment was deposited in a bronze casket of remembrance, together with copies of all the Jubilee programmes, the list of Visiting Officers, a copy of the Annual Report, a set of Jubilee badges, and a copy of the B.B. *Jubilee Bulletin* produced all that week by a national newspaper. The Camp watched in complete silence as the casket was

The Sealed Casket 1933

closed and sealed with wax with the imprint 'B.B. 1933' at one end and 'B.B. 1983' at the other. Many a Boy present at Dechmont that night vowed he would be at the opening of the casket at the Centenary celebrations – fifty years on!

Still the sun shone, every day and all that week. The Jubilee Review took place at Queen's Park Recreation Ground on Saturday 10th September with a parade state of 32,520 Officers and Boys. 100 special trains and as many buses carried the B.B. to Queen's Park where 16 schools were open to provide 1230 breakfasts, 10,949 lunches and 17,700 teas during that long exciting day.

The Inspecting Officer for the great event was His Royal Highness, Prince George, in naval uniform. The Parade of 17 Battalions was led by the 1st Glasgow, under their Captain, Douglas Pearson Smith, son of the Founder. 637 pipers formed the Massed Pipe Bands, all bravely playing 'Highland Laddie'. The most dramatic moment was the Advance in Review order – thousands upon thousands of Boys advancing as one man – over a quarter of the total strength of the Brigade. No wonder Prince George said:

> I want to congratulate every one of you on this parade. Your appearance and efficiency have served to show that the spirit of The Boys' Brigade is stronger than ever. The King warmly

congratulates The Brigade on reaching the fiftieth milestone of its life of valuable service to the youth of our country, and desires me to express His Majesty's best wishes for the continued welfare and prosperity of The Boys' Brigade.

The National Anthem brought the official Review to an end, then cheers upon cheers for their royal visitor, and pill-boxes thrown high in the air. Then, from all over the ground came the rising chorus of the Jubilee Song, from more than 80,000 Boys and spectators more or less in unison:

> For fifty years the work's been done,
> And now it's ours to carry on!

Jubilee Sunday brought the largest open-air service ever held in this country, the Conventicle at Hampden Park, normally the scene of league and international football matches. There were 130,000 men and women, boys and girls and members of the B.B. in the ground, and at least another 100,000 outside, who could not get in. They had to be content with the distant sound from the loudspeakers. The Right Reverend Lauchlan Maclean Watt, poet, preacher and Moderator of the General Assembly of the Church of Scotland, conducted the Service of Worship. His text was, 'Which hope we have

as an anchor of the soul, both sure and stedfast.' And to the Boys he said:

> You are the world-builders, the centuries are growing in your hearts. You are the Children of the Daybreak and the Young Hopefuls of Jesus Christ. So today we thank God for the spiritual genius of William Smith who, building better than he knew, liberated a dream that has been an instrument of blessing for humanity.

The whole great company joined in the old Scottish psalms, 'All people that on earth do dwell' and 'The Lord's my Shepherd'. Everyone, for a mile round about, heard the singing.

Monday brought an excursion on the Firth of Clyde for everyone who had taken part in the Jubilee celebrations. The Boys embarked on the steamers *Duchess of Argyll* and *Jupiter*, the visiting Officers on the *Duchess of Hamilton* and *Queen Mary*, bright with bunting from stem to stern. A long golden day took them by way of the Kyles of Bute and the site of the very first B.B. Camp. Then, on the homeward way, they sang the final chorus of the Jubilee Song and 'Auld Lang Syne'. A splendid Jubilee – a time to look back on fifty glorious years and to look forward with hope to the centenary of The Boys' Brigade. And it was a week of perfect weather, without a drop of rain.

Many organizations for boys and girls followed the pioneer example of William A. Smith and The Boys' Brigade. Among them were The Church Lads' Brigade, The London Diocesan Church Lads' Brigade, The Catholic Boys' Brigade, The Jewish Lads' Brigade, The Boys' Life Brigade and The Boy Scouts. Cadet Corps, boys' clubs, and other youth organizations were to follow.

Parallel organizations for girls were The Girls' Guildry (founded by Dr. W. F. Somerville, a Glasgow B.B. Officer and close friend of William Smith), The Girls' Life Brigade, and The Girl Guides. Further afield was The Boys' Brigade in the British Commonwealth overseas and in the United States of America. The B.B. was also the inspiration for the Danish Boys' Brigade – Frivilligt Drenge-Forbund. The F.D.F. has always kept in friendly touch with their older brothers of the B.B.

YOUNG BROTHERS

Two stalwart members of the F.D.F.

Royal review Windsor Castle 1943

There have been many Royal occasions on which all the British youth organizations have paraded together, but there was never any doubt which was 'First for Boys'. At Windsor Castle in 1943, for instance, during the Diamond Jubilee celebrations, His Majesty King George VI inspected a review of The Boys' Brigade and said:

When The Boys' Brigade was founded sixty years ago, your Founder, Sir William A. Smith, builded better than he knew, for he started not only a great movement, but one from which all our present widespread youth training was destined to spring. Good luck to you and all your comrades! May all you Boys live to see the centenary of this great movement.

The Princess Elizabeth, the King's daughter and future Queen was there to hear her father's words.

The Boys' Life Brigade had a very similar background to the B.B. Their accoutrements were field service cap, belt and haversack, and their badge a crown and the Geneva cross. Their motto was 'To Save Life'. As early as 1914 it had been suggested that the two organizations might unite, but the Council of the B.L.B. could not agree. The insuperable objections were the rifle used in B.B. drill and the fact that some B.B. Companies were associated with the military Cadet Force. Ten years later these difficulties had disappeared. Few mourned the passing of the dummy rifle, least of all the Boys to whom it had become an old-fashioned toy. On 1st October 1926 The Boys' Brigade and The Boys' Life Brigade united. The membership of the B.B. at the time was 1436 Companies and 71,087 Officers and Boys, and of the B.L.B., 654 Companies and 29,473 Officers and Boys.

The newly united organization took the name The Boys' Brigade. The B.B. anchor badge combined neatly with the Geneva cross of the B.L.B. to form their emblem. The Junior name Boy Reserves disappeared, and the cheerful title 'Life Boys' was adopted from the junior league of the B.L.B.

It is astonishing how uniforms have varied through the years for both senior and junior Boys. By and large England hankered after a full uniform, while Scotland stuck obstinately with cap, belt and haversack. It was probably the rigour of clothes rationing in World War II which brought the B.B. back to the simple accoutrements of its earliest days. Haversacks, for example, became as scarce as gold and were washed, ironed, and handed on from one boy to another. The 9th Thames Valley (Kingston) Company launched a Haversack Salvage Campaign to make sure their new recruits were properly outfitted. Another Company bought yards of twill sheeting and persuaded a sympathetic mum to turn them into haversacks. Others used some of the family sheets, or resorted to flour bags. Meanwhile there was a strict directive about B.B. belts: 'Belts are now only supplied on condition – stipulated by The Board of Trade – that they are collected when a Boy leaves and re-issued.' At least it diverted the thinking of the B.B. from the medley of military leggings and other refinements which were sometimes suggested at Council meetings.

The new Life Boys instantly scored a success with boys between 9 and 12. The usual uniform was a Naval-pattern cap with 'The Life Boys' on the ribbon, the lifebelt badge on the left breast, smart blue jersey and shorts, and black stockings with two saxe-blue rings. The whole programme for the younger boy was bright and cheerful, with

Making Christmas decorations

games, singing, figure-marching, hobbies, nature study, and a seal system for competition. They had their own naval style salute. And for the first time women had a part in the Movement. Many a young boy first lost his heart to a bonny girl Leader in her trim uniform. The fact that many of them were trained day school teachers gave them an understanding of the ways of youngsters.

The Life Boys were enthusiasts in everything they did. To give but one example – the missionary movement of the Brigade owes them a great deal in the boys' response to the Christmas Appeal. Rather surprisingly, the Haynes Committee of 1963 recommended that they be brought completely into the Brigade, and at Brigade Council in Edinburgh in 1966 The Life Boys were dissolved – Badge, Leaders, Object, and Salute. From September of that year they were merged in The Boys' Brigade as The Junior Section. Their present uniform is a field service cap with B.B. badge, blue jersey, grey shorts or trousers, and grey stockings. Their four-sided Achievement Scheme is based on Christian Citizenship, and Physical, Educational and Service activities, and the badges to be won shine in white, green, purple, blue, red and gold on the right arm.

To hold the loyalty of the Junior Section is not hard. But what about their little brothers who insist on being noticed? William Smith's judgment was firmly set. His ages were to be 'all boys between the ages of 12 and 17'. He even mentioned a 'standard height' in the early days, 'probably 4'6" '. To take in younger boys meant losing older boys. Smith's aim was to hold the older boys and pass them on to membership of the Church, and perhaps to his beloved Volunteers.

The argument about age has raged ever since. When Brigade Council is not discussing the niceties of uniform it is involved in an argument about 'B.B. age'. But the youngsters won their place, at first unofficially, and then with full approval. The six-year-olds have flocked in to form the Pre-Junior Section, variously known as 'Imps', 'Sparks', 'Shipmates', 'Cabin Boys', 'Robins', 'Anchor Boys', or what you will. Their uniform is a red jersey with sewn B.B. cloth badge and grey trousers. They meet for a play-hour of fun and good company and attend Sunday School or Church Service. The days of the Achievement Scheme, Badges, and the uniformed parades and discipline of The Boys' Brigade are something to look forward to.

The modern plan takes in the following age limits for the whole Brigade:

Pre-Junior Section:	6th birthday to the end of the session in which the Boy reaches 8 years of age.
Junior Section:	8th birthday to the end of the session in which the Boy reaches 12 years of age.

Their very first Display!

Company Section

Company Section	11th birthday to the end of the session in which the Boy reaches 17 years of age. Where a Senior Section does not operate the upper age limit is the end of the session in which the Boys becomes 18 years of age.
Senior Section:	16th birthday to the end of the session in which the Boy becomes 18 years of age.

But, as usual, Sir William Smith was right. The B.B. has more and more lost its Senior Boys. So there will be changes still to come.

It is a curious fact that the Boy who will groan at the very thought of school tests and exams will compete eagerly for awards that mark him out as a smart member of The Boys' Brigade!

The very first emblem of the B.B. was the red rosette patiently sewn by Mrs William A. Smith, wife of the Founder, and worn on the jacket lapel of the captain and his first two lieutenants. The boys themselves, in 1883, were plain as plain could be in their drab Victorian workaday clothes.

Today there are awards and achievements to be aimed at the moment a Boy enrols in the Brigade. The 6 year-old Robin or Anchor Boy of the Pre-Junior Section begins with a cloth badge of the movement on his red jersey. By the time he is in the Juniors at the age of 8 he starts with basic achievements and goes on to the glory of white, green, purple, blue, red and gold awards for an amazing variety of activities. How surprised some parents must be to hear of them! Among 132 'achievements' he may be able to tell the story of a Bible parable, sew on a button, set a table, solve a crossword puzzle, keep his bicycle in a roadworthy state, know his road signs from the Highway Code, name and use simple tools, take part in Kim's Game, run and swim and throw and catch, keep his footing on the ski-slopes, read a compass, identify aircraft and their markings, play a musical instrument, make a good cup of tea, understand a map, and plan a cross-country expedition. There is a place in the Achievement Scheme for the handicapped Boy as for the quickest, each giving of his best.

The teenager in the Company Section takes his awards very seriously. Each Company has its own well-planned programme of activities, physical, educational and spiritual, for every season of the year. The Boy begins with a Target Award to show that he knows what the B.B. is all about. Then the wide world of skill and enthusiasm is open to him: Arts, Crafts and Hobbies Badges, the Camping, Canoeing, Christian Education, and Communications Badges, the Drill Badge, whose device is the chess king, the only piece that can move in any direction one pace at a time! There is an Expedition Badge, a First Aid Badge (the oldest award of the lot, if one remembers the ambulance classes of the early B.B. Companies), an International Badge, Life-Saving Badge, Naturalist's Badge, Physical Recreation Badge, Safety Badge, Sailing Badge, Seamanship Badge, Swimming Badge, and Sportsman's Colours for skill in any activity from Archery to Table Tennis, summed up in the badge bearing the device of the laurel wreath to depict the all-rounder.

The older Boy knows that the President's Badge is a special award

Awards and Achievements

70

Indoors and out of doors

71

for which he must be specially recommended by his Company Captain after gaining a number of other awards. And highest of all, and greatly to be coveted, is the Queen's Badge for Boys who have shown knowledge and understanding of The Boys' Brigade at every level, practical leadership in the Company, and who commit themselves to some service for others in the community.

So the final glory of a Senior Boy will be an immaculate turn-out of cap, belt and haversack, buttonhole badge of membership, and his hard-won badges on armlets worn thus:

Left Arm:	top row	:	Queen's Badge
	centre row	:	President's Badge
	bottom row	:	Gold Achievement Badge
			Brigade Service Badge
Right Arm:	top row	:	Target Award
	additional	:	specialized awards, worn in
	rows		alphabetical order, not more than
			seven in a row.

Such a Boy, in full parade uniform, has made the most of his years and service in The Boys' Brigade.

There was a time when he would have been well aware of the weight of glory and responsibility, especially on his right arm. Until recently, badges were made of frosty-silver nickel and each weighed 6 grams. Today, in high impact polystyrene they are brighter than ever, and much lighter at 2 grams apiece.

Sir William Smith described promotion to NCO as the greatest honour for a B.B. Boy. The NCO is the best-disciplined Boy on parade, trained in the ceremonial of Colour parties, competent as instructor, squad commander and leader, friend and example to the younger Boys. The Founder's basic rule was that the NCO should know the Brigade from A to Z and should be its finest representative of true Christian manliness.

The awards, achievements and badges of The Boys' Brigade have changed considerably in design and appearance through the century. Some lie about in tins and boxes, the proud souvenirs of members of days gone by. They may well become a collector's treasure-trove. Who, for example, remembers and possesses the Old Boys' Union Badge, engraved on the back with name, Company, and years of service, and intended to be worn on the watch chain? Or the five pointed star? Or the Service Badges of both World Wars? And what of the Jubilee Badge of 1933 and the special buttonhole badge issued only to Boys who attended the Dechmont Camp? There is also the

The Colour Party

Founder's Camp Badge of 1954, as well as special badges for the Coronation of King George VI and the Coronation of Queen Elizabeth II, the Investiture of the Prince of Wales, and the Queen's Silver Jubilee. These, and many like them, are keepsakes for days to come.

One high award of recent years has still to be mentioned. It is the Duke of Edinburgh's Award, introduced in 1956 by His Royal Highness Prince Philip himself, 'to encourage and stimulate the

73

London Boys set out for International Camp, Kingston, Jamaica, 1958. The breast badge was specially designed for this camp.

enthusiasms and energies of young people between the ages of 14 and 25 in the United Kingdom and throughout the Commonwealth'. The Boys' Brigade, as the senior of all youth organizations, had the honour to be asked to be a pilot organization when the Award was instituted, since when it has become the premier achievement in all that is finest in citizenship, adventure and service.

The Duke of Edinburgh Award may be gained in Bronze, Silver or Gold, and all young people who take part have to meet the strict requirements of four sections: Service, Expeditions, Skills, and Physical Recreation. The Award is not competitive. For the member of the B.B. it is a challenge to be the very best a Boy can be.

The one rare distinction that remains is the Cross for Heroism which was introduced in 1902 and is given only for an act of bravery where a Boy puts his own life at risk for others, or who has displayed marked courage in face of danger. It is the V.C. of Brigade Awards. Since it was first instituted 191 Crosses have been gained. Five of them were awarded to Boys whose heroism cost them their young lives.

*   *   *

Written examinations for awards are a serious matter. In the examination for the Camper's Badge one boy wrote: 'There should be a pit dug for the cook, about six feet long, three feet deep.'

*Review of Duke of Edinburgh
Award Scheme with H.R.H. The
Duke of Edinburgh observing*

*Simon Herriott, aged 9, winner of the
Boys' Brigade Cross for Heroism*

Far Round The World

Founder's Camp Eton College 1954: Danish Boys meet Boys from Neenah, Wisconsin.

Only a few years after the first meeting in a back street in Glasgow, we find the B.B. established in the new world of the United States of America. It was a very different scene. In the USA, Sabbath School Halls were usually comfortably carpeted. How could they cope with healthy, hearty Boys drilling up and down? Professor Henry Drummond, friend of the Founder and tireless enthusiast for all things B.B., gave his opinion: 'a yard of Boy is worth fifty yards of carpet!' So the new movement flourished, and went on to become 'The United Boys' Brigades of America.' Perhaps they had an early tendency 'to run into gold braid, white gloves, cocked hats, feathers, and so on'. But today they apply themselves in true B.B. spirit to work for the Christian Education Badge, the Drill Badge, and Camping, Expedition and Sports Badges.

A lively picture of the pioneer American days is to be seen in a description of one of the early Camps of the 1st San Francisco Company. It was held at Inverness, a remote spot in the Californian mountains by the side of a lake, beyond the forests of pine and redwood. The Boys at once 'unlimbered their guns and went off in search of game', and their days at camp were occupied in hunting, fishing, boating, swimming and, of course, eating. No dummy rifles there! 'That the Boys did justice to the plain but wholesome fare is evidenced by the fact that during the encampment they ate 11,800

loaves of bread, 2100 rolls, 275 pies, 4400 pounds of meat, 150 dollars worth of groceries, 66 dollars worth of butter and eggs, and drank 50 dollars worth of milk.' Some Company! Some Country!

By the year 1889 there were already Companies in New Zealand, always one of the keenest B.B. regions of the world. The tireless Professor Drummond took himself off on a lecture tour of Australia with a specimen of The Boys' Brigade cap, belt and haversack and a large supply of B.B. literature, and in no time at all Melbourne was writing to William Smith in Glasgow for application forms, member-

Company activities in New Zealand

Far round the world

ship cards and order forms for equipment. Today, Australia, New Zealand and Nigeria are, outside Britain, the three most populous B.B. countries in the world.

There was soon a B.B. Company in South Africa, the 1st Natal, consisting of Zulu Boys, and in Europe, long before the EEC, there was a 1st Brussels Company in Belgium. Canada and the West Indies also wore the B.B. uniform and there was an early Company in Calcutta, with Boys who were Indians, Jews, Eurasian, Burmese, Japanese and African.

Today you may spin the globe and find the B.B. almost everywhere. A body known as The World Conference binds together The Boys' Brigade of more than sixty countries of the world, as well as brother and sister organizations of similar aims and methods. You may, for example, join the B.B. at camp in the Solomon Islands, build your own leafy shelter, and enjoy an open-air supper of rice, sweet potato and fish fresh from the lagoon. In Papua New Guinea the Boys will be on trek through the tropical forest or splashing within the sweep of coral reefs along a coconut fringed shore. On parade they wear a distinctive sash and cap and go barefoot. And there are Companies to visit in the Cook Islands, Samoa, Bermuda, Belize, Haiti, Jamaica, the Bahamas, St. Kitts, and Anguilla. You need an atlas and a chart to find them all, and an island-hopping plane, but there will always be a B.B. welcome.

The Boys' Brigade has flourished from the beginning in West Africa. In Sierra Leone, Ghana, Cameroon, and especially in Nigeria (with a membership of over 70,000) where they are planning a National Headquarters in Lagos with a training centre, a camp house and a sports area. On the other side of that vast continent full-time B.B. workers serve the movement in Uganda, Kenya, Zimbabwe and in Zambia, where they have an agricultural project for Boys to encourage them to grow vegetables, rear chickens, and plant fruit trees – pawpaw, orange, guava, tangerine, mangoes and avocado pears – all for sale in the local market. In the poor but lovely mountain country of Lesotho a boy learns to herd cattle almost as soon as he can walk. One of the B.B. groups meets regularly at the cathedral in Maseru, the capital.

Australia's widely scattered Companies meet not only in the great modern cities such as Sydney, Melbourne, Adelaide, Perth, Brisbane, but also in faraway outposts with romantic names such as Nhulumbuy, Casurina, and Elcho Island in the Gulf of Carpentaria. The Pan-Australian Camps of The Boys' Brigade 'down under' are the envy of the whole movement.

The Brigade in the vast sweep of coast-to-coast Canada takes in the romantic Salmon Arm in British Columbia, Frobisher Bay at the top of the world, and Pictou and Cape Breton in Nova Scotia. The name for The Boys' Brigade in the Eskimo tongue is Sorusikattigerk, but the programme is universally B.B. – drill, songs, music-making, stories, handicrafts, games, and, in the forefront, 'the advancement of Christ's Kingdom among Boys'.

In Asia there are B.B. Companies in India and Bangladesh, in Malaysia, 'the land below the wind', Brunei and Hong Kong. It was Lance-Corporal Goh See Choon, aged 14, of the 1st Seremban Company, Malaya, who noted that the volcanic island of Krakatoa, between Sumatra and Java, erupted in the year 1883. It was so violent that the noise was heard in Australia, over 2000 miles away. Clouds of dust particles brought about vivid sunsets all over the world for the next three years. But that 1883 explosion, said Goh See Choon, was as nothing to the founding of the B.B. the same year and its effect spreading across the world to Singapore, 10,000 miles away!

The history of the Brigade in Singapore is a tale of courage and triumph in dark and evil days. It was an Aberdonian called James M. Fraser who set the B.B. in Singapore, the island outpost of Empire at the very tip of Asia. Fraser was Boy, NCO and Staff Sergeant in the 23rd Aberdeen, and he never left the B.B. all his life long. At the age of 20, as a qualified architect, he was in Singapore, on the other side of the world, with the promise to his former B.B. Captain that he would start a Company as soon as he could set about it. And so he did, with a first meeting of twelve Chinese Boys and Drill and Bible Class from the beginning. The Boys saved up penny by penny, week by week until they had a full uniform of blue shirt and shorts and blue stockings. They had their own gymnastic classes and tumbling teams and singles sticks and their first concert and display, and all, as Fraser said, 'the way I was trained to do it in Aberdeen!'

James M. Fraser made a point of meeting the ships from home that came in to the bustling port and immediately got in touch with any likely B.B. Officers who had come out to the Colony to work. So, in a short time there was a second Company, and a third, a fourth, a fifth, and in no time at all, a Battalion, with their first President, James M. Fraser. We have already heard of the two Singapore Boys, Choy Ah Soo and Tan Keng Kang who saved up to come to the Jubilee in Glasgow in 1933. Both Boys were in their final year at school and facing important exams, so Fraser made them promise to study for at least an hour every day all through their travels and the Jubilee celebrations in the West!

Calamity came in 1942 with the fall of Singapore to the Japanese, the worst single disaster in the history of the British Empire. Choy Ah Soo was only one of many loyal Chinese lined up on the beach and shot. James M. Fraser had been a Volunteer from the very day he arrived in Singapore as a young man – he did nothing by half – and at the outbreak of war he was in charge of the Singapore Searchlight Battery. With the fall of the city he was a prisoner of war for three and a half years in the horrors of Changi Jail and other Japanese prison camps. Even there, lying weak and sick with dysentery, he made secret contact with B.B. Boys and B.B. Officers, devising membership cards for a Stedfast Club from scraps of paper.

In Singapore the B.B. disappeared completely under the grim occupation of the Japanese. The Battalion Colours were burned to prevent their being desecrated by the enemy. They hid away their band instruments. When the great day of liberation came, out came the bugles and drums to be polished and refurbished, and when Fraser returned from his years in the prison camp the Battalion came to life again, with almost all the old Companies. Within three months he led a Battalion Church Parade at St. Andrew's Cathedral. In 1980 The Boys' Brigade in Singapore celebrated their half-century, and without a doubt they will send representatives to the centenary celebrations in Glasgow. If you want to know what 'Sure and Stedfast' means, take a look at Singapore, and thank God for men like James M. Fraser.

The last place one would expect to find The Boys' Brigade is the vast mysterious land of China. In fact, the first Company was founded 68 years ago in Swatow, South China, by a missionary, the Rev. A. Guthrie Gamble, who was a former Captain of the 6th Cambridge. It was the first of eight Companies in the South China Battalion, in a land of earthquake, typhoon, famine, flood, and constant warfare. Many of the B.B. Boys came to Swatow from the Philippines, the Malay Peninsula, and even Java, 2000 miles away.

We have only a fleeting glimpse of the Chinese B.B. in days of persecution. The Communists began a fierce anti-Christian campaign – church buildings were burned down and worship forbidden, B.B. Headquarters looted and their records destroyed. The Boys stood firm to their faith, but torture and killings followed. In the world story of the Brigade, China is a memory of martyrdom. Even the very name Swatow has vanished from the atlas. But tomorrow, in the vast land of China, in God's time, who knows?

The biggest B.B. Company in the world has 827 Boys and 308

leaders – 1135 members in all. It is the Neenah-Menasha twin-city Company in Wisconsin, USA. One night in the fall of 1899 a local Presbyterian minister found half a dozen boys on the steps of the small town hall. They had no business to be out – the curfew sounded nightly because of the Spanish-American War – but they told the minister they wanted an 'army' of their own. The Rev. Dr. Chapin said he would see what he could do. He knew the B.B. Aim and Object as William Smith had set it out in Scotland. So the B.B. in Neenah-Menasha began on 21st January 1900 with some men of the community helping with drill and games. One of them, S. Frank Shattuck promised to give a hand 'for a few months'. In all, he served for 56 years and came to be known to generation after generation of Boys as 'father' of the Company.

At first they had various homes – a roller-skating rink, a warehouse, a gymnasium, a creamery. Nowadays they have a splendid building of their own with a completely equipped gym, basketball court and showers, assembly room and side-rooms with woodworking machinery, radio and photographic equipment and a library. A complete description of the Neenah-Menasha annual programme would fill a book, with news of their camp, hunting and fishing clubs, rifle team, and hobbies of every kind. Its Christian tradition makes the Company the only one of its kind in the USA, with the strict rule that a Boy must maintain regular attendance at his own church or Sunday School, and the original B.B. motto at the heart of all their work – 'The advancement of Christ's Kingdom among Boys'.

To round off The World Conference one must mention the brother and sister organizations which have grown up from the inspiration of The Boys' Brigade. Best known of these is the FDF/FPF. The FDF – Frivilligt-Drenge-Forbund – which began in a suburb of Copenhagen in October 1902, has an Aim and Object which is a literal translation of the B.B. Aim. FPF is the similar organization for girls, and between them they form Denmark's largest Christian Youth Organization, with more than 40,000 members. Many a British B.B. Company has been made welcome at Camp in Denmark, and the FDF are always smartly on parade as guests at every notable B.B. celebration.

In Sweden there is the Ansgarsforbundet, a uniformed organization for boys and girls within the national Church, and in Finland, Poikien Keskus, which is an organization of boys' clubs in the Evangelical Lutheran Church. The boys have no uniforms, but there are emblems and badges, a hiking centre in Finnish Lapland, and 62,000 eager members.

The World Conference began with The Boys' Brigade and every year sees it reach farther and farther round the globe as a worldwide movement of Christian fellowship and service among young people. They have in mind the lines of the B.B. hymn:

> In Christ there is no East or West,
> In Him no South or North,
> But one great fellowship of love
> Throughout the whole wide earth.

Every good B.B. Officer and Boy knows that The Boys' Brigade belongs to Glasgow. It was William Smith himself who saw further. He called London 'the centre of our national life', and as early as 1885 a Company Captain who was also an Anglican vicar was appointed Assistant Brigade Secretary to look after the Movement's interests in the capital. The Founder knew that he could not greatly interest the Established Church of England in the B.B. from distant and Presbyterian Scotland. By the time of the glorious Diamond Jubilee of 1897, William Smith had diligently encouraged archbishop and bishops, field-marshals and generals, university professors and Lord Mayors to lend their names and influence to the Brigade. A dutiful address was presented to Her Majesty as 'a tribute of Esteem, Loyalty and Affection', and His Royal Highness the Duke of

Paternoster Row to Parsons Green

Cornwall and York became the first Royal Patron of The Boys' Brigade. Public meetings and Demonstrations were held regularly in London and were soon to culminate in the Albert Hall Display as the crowning event of the B.B. Year. All that remained was to have a permanent home in 'the Metropolis of Empire'.

Facts and figures supported the move. By the turn of the century considerably more than half the membership of the B.B. was in England, Wales and the Channel Islands. So, in 1902, the London

On the Horseguards Parade in London

Office of the Brigade was opened in Paternoster House, 34 Paternoster Row, under the shadow of St. Paul's Cathedral, with a cobbled entrance and posts to stop anything but horses, and Mr Roger S. Peacock was appointed full-time London Secretary. Church and civic dignitaries approved. So also did the London street urchins with their chant:

> Here comes The Boys' Brigade
> All smovered in marmalade;
> A tuppenny ha'penny pill box
> And half a yard of braid!

Within another session there were a hundred Companies in London alone.

It was about this time that the B.B. *Gazette* discussed two matters concerning the Boys. One was the curious fact that in spite of constant admonitions about smartness of turnout, freshly-laundered haversacks, gleaming belts and polished boots, nothing was ever said at Camp about B.B. Boys cleaning their teeth. Apparently the practice was almost unknown. So said Arnold Wilson, the Brigade Treasurer. Before long, however, the Captain of the 1st Hartlepool wrote to say that his Company provided every Boy with a toothbrush, bought wholesale for one penny each, 'and twice a day, after the morning service of biscuits, and after prayers, before the Boys retire for the night, each Boy takes a mug filled with water by the Fatigue Squad and on the bugle sounding "Commence Firing", sets to work vigorously with his brush'.

The other worthy piece of advice offered by the *Gazette* was entitled Hints to Working Lads':

1. No young man has any right to ask a girl to marry him until he is in a position to offer her a comfortable home. Under present social conditions, this will not, as a rule, be until he is 25 years of age at least.
2. During his apprenticeship, a self-respecting lad will hand *all* his earnings to his mother, getting back so much for pocket money.
3. The remaining five shillings would be lodged as a sacred trust, each week, say, in the Post Office Savings Bank.
4. In choosing the girl who is to be your wife, remember you are not simply choosing one who will do you credit when 'walking out' or as a partner in a dance, but one who is to be a help-meet all through life. You want one,

then, whose qualities will last, who will make a thrifty housewife, and a good mother to your children, healthy, therefore, and from a good home, of similar tastes to yourself, and of the same religion, not to be found often on the street, but modest; not cheapening herself, but keeping you at your proper distance; one whom to woo and win is worth your while.

The union with The Boys' Life Brigade clinched 'the London matter' by almost doubling the size of the Movement. The B.L.B. with their Junior League, The Life Boys, had an Aim and Object very similar to the senior organization, with their emphasis on training 'for an active, disciplined and useful manhood'. They used the same worthy Victorian terms such as 'habits of self-respect, obedience, courtesy, helpfulness to others and all that makes for a manly Christian character'. They, too, had drill, but they absolutely abhorred the use of the rifle. Their motto was: 'To save life', and their exercises were aimed at rescue from fire, from drowning and from accident. When the B.B. at last agreed to get rid of their dummy rifles, nothing stood in the way of union, and it was a happy one from the beginning.

The London Office was now too small, so a move was made to Abbey House, Westminster, just across the road from the Abbey and the Mother of Parliaments. One could hardly get nearer the heart of Empire than that! It was formally agreed by Brigade Council that 'the Brigade Secretary should make his headquarters in London', so, when G. Stanley Smith moved south from Glasgow in 1930, Abbey House became the national and international headquarters of the Brigade. Glasgow opened new and spacious offices at 168 Bath Street and appointed the notable Andrew Macpherson to be Battalion and Scottish Secretary.

The 1930s proved to be 'the golden age of the B.B.' The Jubilee of 1933 was, of course, the highlight, when the Camp at Dechmont, the Review in Queen's Park, Glasgow, and the Conventicle at Hampden brought together the largest gathering of Officers and Boys ever seen in the United Kingdom. But there were other notable advances during that decade. In 1933, for example, William H. McVicker came to London from Belfast as Life Boys and Overseas Secretary of The Boys' Brigade. He was to be the best-known and best-loved B.B. man in the world for more than thirty years as the Brigade went from strength to strength in every continent.

Another advance of the '30s was the beginning of Training Schools for Officers. New ways for leaders were very much needed. The old-style B.B. had relied on Officers who had trained in the Volunteers or who had served in the Forces. Now the contentious rifle was at last abandoned, the Boys were no longer 'marching as to war' and the whole Movement was inclined to seek more diverse and open-air activities than could be found in the drill hall. A Training Centre was opened at 'Bolobo' in Edgeware, Middlesex, a house that took its colourful name from a Baptist Mission Station in the Belgian Congo. Scotland had its training, camping and recreation centre at Balrossie, in Renfrewshire. In 1936 no fewer than six Brigade training schools were held, and about the same time B.B. Organizers and full-time Training Officers were being appointed up and down the country.

World War II saw the original office at Paternoster House destroyed by an enemy bomb, and Abbey House stood at the very heart of German air raids over London. The B.B. Ambulance Handbook sold over 200,000 copies because the Home Office recommended it as the best handbook on First Aid available. Night after night the headquarters staff were on fire watch on the flat roof looking over the River Thames, alert under the continuous gunfire, the drone of planes and the crash of bombs dropping along the crowded riverside. The office boy, aged 16, was Kenneth Wiggins, known as 'Wiggs', a member of a London Company of the B.B. Kenneth was on duty with the A.R.P. Service many nights during the heavy bombing. On a bright September morning, a day of victory for the R.A.F., he set out on his bike for work as usual, the air raid sirens sounding as he started. The guns roared, but Wiggs rode on. The bombs fell on that stricken London street, and Wiggs was a wartime casualty, with no memorial to mark his passing. He was one of the unsung heroes of those days, on duty to the end.

Black-out, evacuation, air raids and other hazards brought a dramatic wartime fall in B.B. membership. Officers, Warrant Officers and Staff-Sergeants volunteered or were called up to the Forces. Senior Boys gave their services at First Aid Posts, in the Auxiliary Fire Service, and in air raid precautions and rescue work. The first Distinguished Flying Cross of the war was presented personally by King George VI to Flying Officer Drew Macpherson, son of the Glasgow Battalion Secretary. Drew was a B.B. Officer in the 32nd Glasgow Company. Not long after, he was reported missing, believed killed.

The 4th Jersey Company in the Channel Islands carried on in defiance of the occupying Nazi authority. They had their Company parades in secret every Thursday and Band practice every Tuesday in spite of threats by the German forces. On 9th May 1945, there came the end of the occupation and the unconditional surrender of German troops in Jersey and throughout the Channel Islands. At 11.30 that morning there came a message from the Bailiff of Jersey to warn the Old Boys' Band to appear in the Royal Square early next morning. They were on parade to a man.

Across the channel, a solitary B.B. Company, the 1st Amsterdam, kept going in great difficulty. The blitzkreig which fell on Holland brought devastation to the cities, and there was harsh repression and persecution. Towards the end of the war sheer starvation was common. 'We have eaten potato peelings and tulip bulbs. No milk, no cheese, no fat or butter, no meat or vegetables – all gone to Germany. No gas, electricity or radio, no trams. Our bicycles were stolen and our cars, lorries, railway engines and coaches. Holland is empty and poor.' Some of the sturdiest of the B.B. Boys were taken to force labour in Germany. But, camouflaged as the 'Jongens Gilde' the B.B. struggled to carry on.

In brighter post-war days the B.B. set itself to new tasks for a new generation. Felden Lodge, the Brigade Training Centre in Hertfordshire, opened on 22nd October 1949, bought with funds given to the B.B. by the South Africa Aid to Britain Fund in recognition of the British people's courage during the years of war. Carronvale in

Mr. George Thomas,
Speaker of the House of Commons,
himself an Old Boy of the B.B.
and our Hon. Vice-President

89

Larbert, at the heart of Scotland, was opened as the Scottish Training Centre, and later Rathmore House in Ireland.

Post-war B.B. activities showed new life in the Brigade at home and abroad. These were the days of celebration of the centenary of the Founder's birth, the first B.B. International Camp at Eton, the Duke of Edinburgh's Award, a royal review at Balmoral Castle, the formation of Junior, Company and Senior Sections, and the appointment of Lord Bruce, now the Earl of Elgin, as President of The Boys' Brigade. The B.B. was the first organization ever to organize a sponsored walk – from London to Brighton at a penny a mile – and to raise a handsome sum for Oxfam by doing so.

There were many changes in the new age of the Welfare State. The B.B., like the general population, was moving from the streets of the inner cities to the community centres of the new towns and outlying council estates. 'Membership fluctuated during an era of Teddy Boys, affluence and television, in a permissive society which was becoming more and more materialistic, no longer taking either authority or religion for granted.' It was not easy to be 'Sure and Stedfast' to the high ideal of 'a true Christian manliness'.

In these restless days it was time also to find a new home for the Movement. All sorts of sites were explored up and down London –

The Earl of Elgin and Kincardine, President of the Boys' Brigade, with Seniors from Tyneside

90

derelict churches, warehouses, office blocks, vacant bombed sites. The present Brigade House at Parsons Green was the happy final choice for the joint use of The Boys' Brigade and its sister organization, The Girls' Brigade. From Brigade House the headquarters staff oversee the administration, finances, supplies and training of the whole Movement throughout the United Kingdom. Parsons Green looks out on a grassy common which gives the district its name. It goes back through the centuries to 'P'songrene' of the late 14th century, when the rector of the parish had a bowling green for the diversion of himself and his staff.

Brigade House at Parsons Green was officially opened on 9th December 1966 by Princess Alexandra, deputizing for Her Majesty the Queen. At its opening Her Majesty wrote:

> I believe that in a swinging age it is still important to have a basis of faith and discipline in order to keep one's feet on the ground. To both Brigades I wish continued dedication and success in their task which serves both Church and Nation.

The official opening of
Brigade House, Parsons Green

In The Name of Christ

The Boys' Brigade is a Christian organization, so it rightly has a worldwide missionary concern. From the very beginning, Bible Class talks and Church Parade services reminded the Boys in the homeland of less fortunate people all round the globe. Those were the days when they sang:

> From Greenland's icy mountains,
> From India's coral strand,
> Where Afric's sunny fountains
> Roll down their golden sand.

Their prize award books by R.M. Ballantyne and G.A. Henty fired the imagination with tales of the outposts of Empire. Magic lantern slides brought faraway scenes before their very eyes. News flowed in

from every corner of the world of dedicated missionary doctors, preachers and engineers who spent their lives in healing and helping the millions in distant lands who had as yet no wealth or learning or trained skills of their own. The missionary in his lonely mud hut was as much a hero in those days as the imperial soldier or the jungle trail-blazer.

The British Empire has long since gone to the pages of the history books. Today we speak of the commonwealth of nations, the ecumenical Church, and the worldwide family of man. But the missionary interest has never failed in The Boys' Brigade. Indeed, it burns today more brightly than ever, if one is to judge by the facts of interest, offerings and volunteers.

Surprisingly enough, one of the first B.B. missionary efforts on record was started by the lively 1st San Francisco Company, which had its own Missionary Society from the start, taking in all its members. 'One hundred dollars each year is fixed as the least amount which the members expect to contribute to Missions.'

Within the British Isles we find the flame of missionary concern alight in every branch of the Church. The Founder said: 'We can imagine nothing more in keeping with our Object', and at an Officers' Conference in Dublin as early as 1895 there was a discussion on 'The Boys' Brigade as a Missionary Auxiliary'. F.C. Carey Longmore, pioneer in many B.B. ventures, spoke about Boys giving a regular halfpenny a week to the Company missionary box.

The Church Missionary Society has counted on enthusiastic B.B. support for almost a century, particularly in medical work. In the year 1890 the 13th London Company was officered by two brothers, Herbert Lankester, Captain, and Arthur Lankester, Lieutenant. Both were doctors. Two years later, Dr. Arthur Lankester went out as a medical missionary to take charge of the C.M.S. hospital at Amritsar, the legendary holy city of the Sikhs in North India. His letters home fired the Boys to have a share in his work. Their first venture was to pay for 'a Boys' Brigade cot at £6 a year'. The news spread and before the year was out other Companies were vying with one another to raise money for other cots and beds. So the B.B. branch of the C.M.S. was born. Yet another Lankester brother, Cecil, became the first Secretary and then followed his two brothers into missionary work. Since their pioneer days the C.M.S. branch has supported hospital beds not only in India, but also in China, Persia (now Iran), Egypt, Palestine and Africa both East and West, and today that work goes on more vigorously than ever before.

During the great missionary era at the turn of the 19th century, The Boys' Brigade played its own part in the work of the London Missionary Society in China, South India, and the Cook Islands of the South Pacific. The Methodist Missionary Society, too, provided a roll call of romantic names: Sarenga, Hankow, Montego Bay, Uzuakoli. In Dichpali in India the B.B. camp was held in a mango grove and every Boy was a leper. At Ijebu in Nigeria, W.F. Mellor, a life-long B.B. Boy and Officer, kept up a constant flow of letters to the Methodist Companies at home. His work was a daily witness to the grace of Christ.

The B.B. Boys of the Presbyterian Church in Ireland have given their support to the work of an Indian doctor in a Church hospital in India, a water supply for a hospital in Malawi, and a farming centre in Gujarat.

The B.B. Baptist World Mission Committee has skilful ways of capturing the interest of the Boys year after year. One year they provide radio transceiver sets for to-and-fro communication in Zaïre, the next they tackle 'Operation Speedboat' to raise funds for outboard motors for dug-out canoes on a tropical river. Their Junior Section Christmas gifts down the years have included a boat for Brazil, Landrovers for Zaïre, bungalows in Bangladesh and gifts to maintain Christian witness in the Caribbean.

The Republic of Brazil occupies half of South America, an area of more than three and a quarter million square miles, almost as big as the whole of Europe. One of the most unusual B.B. missionary ventures in the world is among the shoeshine boys of Pato Branco in Brazil. The Baptist missionary has formed them into a Company, the first in Brazil, with a T-shirt uniform emblazoned with the anchor emblem. Not an orthodox cap, belt and haversack Company, it is true, but they are proud to preserve the letters 'B.B.' in their title: 'Batalhao de Bandeira', the Portuguese for 'Brigade of the Flag' and their motto is unmistakable: 'Firma E Segura' ('Sure and Stedfast').

Christian missionaries were a Scottish export even before the start of the B.B. century. David Livingstone was already a national hero and a legend to every boy by the year 1883. So in the early days of the B.B. we find Scottish Companies contributing to missionary work in Lovedale, South Africa, and Jalna in the heart of India. But the whole-hearted missionary venture which has surpassed all others in Britain began only forty years ago. In 1943 The Boys' Brigade and Life Boys of Scotland took up the idea of having a missionary of their own in Africa. They chose a primitive district in the forests of Nigeria, West Africa, where the missionary lived in a mud-brick house on the left bank of the Cross River. The village was called Apiapum. In those days there were no roads in that part of Nigeria, only twisting tracks, a foot wide, winding from village to village through the undergrowth of the forest and along the farm patches the villagers had cleared for their yams and cassava. The only way to get about was on foot or by dug-out canoe on the river highway.

That first year the Church of Scotland Companies and Teams raised the modest sum of £85 from the whole of Scotland. Then a splendid team of B.B. men formed a Missionary Committee. They launched

On the Cross River, Nigeria

a Life Boy Christmas appeal and each Boy took a card round his friends with a sketch of the Cross River on it, divided into thirty squares, worth threepence each. The donations shot up to a thousand pounds. The missionary sent 'Letters from a Log Canoe' several times a year to be circulated to every Company and Team all over Scotland. They told of his daily work and adventures, the hippos and wild life of the river and tropical forest, the needs of Apiapum and many another African village, and the stories of boys like themselves in that part of West Africa. In no time at all the name Apiapum was known to Boys from the Shetlands to the Borders and their givings grew from year to year. It is a proud memory of the writer of this centenary book that he was that pioneer B.B. missionary. Within four years the

95

Foreign Mission Committee decided they could support another missionary, this time the colourful and heroic figure of Dr. Ahmed Affara and his hospital at Sheikh Othman in Arabia.

The Scottish B.B. venture has grown and grown. Contributions have risen by thousands of pounds, and then by tens of thousands. Every year the B.B. cheque is handed over at a special ceremony to the Moderator of the General Assembly of the Church of Scotland in the name of all the Boys of Scotland. In 1983, amidst the centenary celebrations, the cheque is for £50,000 to aid medical work, agriculture, education, child welfare and evangelism in the lands of Africa, India, and the palm-fringed islands of the West Indies. It is given, like all B.B. missionary offerings, in the name of the Christ of every clime and coast.

The Boys' Brigade of the early years had a winter session of drill and club room, a weekly parade night and Sunday morning Bible class, and a glorious week of Camp to look forward to each summer. Today, the B.B. has moved out of the church hall of its origins into the wider community and the open air. It enjoys a diversity of activities all round the year and all round the world.

Here are some glimpses of the B.B. Year. It starts, as it always did, in the month of September. And what better tune-up for the Session than the stirring sound of the band? The first of all B.B. bands, in William Smith's original company, was a flute band of 16 performers and the instructor was a former band-sergeant of the regular army. In a year or two there were bugle, brass, drum and fife, and pipe-bands. Today, an annual inspection or display would be almost unthinkable without the brave sound of brass and pipes and drums.

ALL ROUND THE YEAR

Making music

Nothing will draw a crowd quicker, or welcome Royalty with more loyal tribute. What small boy has not envied the glory of the big drum with its leopard-skin apron and tornado of sound?

Proficiency in the band leads to badges, prizes and trophies. It is not surprising that the booklet *Bugle calls and marches*, priced 6d., remained in print for nearly fifty years.

*Sponsored Events and
Community Service*

A few years ago, new instruments were added to the traditional military-style bugles, pipes and drums – the trumpet, bell lyra, tympani, cymbals, bongo drums, triple timp-toms and timbales. The Drum-Major adds white gauntlets and sash to the uniform of his rank and twirls and flings his premier mace in magnificent arcs. The ultimate prize in the B.B. Trumpet Band world is to be named Supreme Champions in the National Marching Bands Contest. It appeals especially to the Senior Boy. All young people respond instinctively to rhythm, and the sight and sound of a marching band in full accoutrements and equipment truly lifts the heart. The marching band has also brought a new and lively style of drill, not always approved by the old brigade. But one must remember that formal drill is largely out of date, even in the modern Armed Forces. The marching band combines attractive, disciplined and healthful physical movement with the sheer joy of rhythm and skill of tune.

The Awards structure involves Boys in the needs of the community. Christian service is not a vague impulse for do-goodery. It is a disciplined life-skill for helping and caring. So B.B. Boys up and down the land volunteer for work in children's homes, Special Schools and general hospitals. They visit physically handicapped children and share in their games, and do cheerful work for elderly folk who can no longer look after their own gardens or decorate their homes. The open-air awards for Queen's Men take in life saving, cave

101

B.B. Week

rescue, mountain leader training and many other service tasks. The Boys keep a diary to show the duties they have chosen and the times and details of their commitment. Service is the watchword, and its patient days and weeks and months lead a Boy to notice and to ponder the many and changing needs of the community where he lives.

The Achievement Scheme for Junior Sections has the same aim. For example, as part of his social achievements a Boy may come to know something of the life of a handicapped person by regular visiting over a period of time, or write to a society which specializes in a particular handicap and produce a scrapbook with press cuttings, pictures, writing, and detailed information. A number of B.B. Companies have special sections for mentally handicapped and physically handicapped Boys.

In a very different part of the B.B. world, September in Lesotho is the beginning of Spring, and the B.B. Organizer sets out through the morning frost to visit villages in the white-capped mountain country.

October brings Founder's Day which commemorates the birth of William A. Smith in Thurso on 27th October 1854.

'B.B. Supplies' are fully stocked in more than 25 centres up and down the country, with everything from buttonhole badges to

103

complete uniforms for every shape and size of Boy or Officer. Brigade House has to point out that some training in jersey drill is needed:

> Try an experiment in your Junior and Pre-Junior Section. Ask the Boys to pretend to remove their jerseys and then stop them. It's the Boys you find who are gripping the neck of the garment who are doing the damage. Mums don't always teach them the correct way, which is to cross the arms in front, grip the bottom hem in both hands and then pull the jersey up and over the head.

Meanwhile, in the tropical forest of Cameroon it is raining heavily, but the B.B. are on parade as usual. Find them on the map!

November used to be memorable in the B.B. Company for 'B.B. Week' when the Boys raised money for the continuing work of the Movement by going round their relatives and friends with collecting cards. It was an idea of R.S. Peacock, former H.Q. Secretary and Captain of the 76th London Company, just after the first World War. Nowadays the boys themselves prefer to put their loyalty, ingenuity and enthusiasm to good use by a great variety of sponsored events – all night non-stop table tennis or badminton, sponsored silence, marathon wood chops, car washing, a mile of pennies in the high street, hill-climbs, and countless other activities of every imaginable and unimaginable kind.

In Finland's Poikien Keskus the boys and their leader are planning their weekly club meeting – games, arts and crafts, acting, discussions, Bible reading and prayers. Meanwhile, on the B.B. farm in Zambia, the mangoes and avocado pears are ripening fast.

In December, B.B. Companies keep Christmas with 'Operation Goodwill': food parcels for old folk, a Christmas party at the children's home, carol services in hospital wards and old people's homes. Down under in New Zealand it is high summer and the B.B. are under canvas, with canoes on the fast-flowing rivers for Seniors and hill walking for the Juniors.

The turn of the year brings competitions, parents' evenings and preparation for the annual Inspection and Display, as well as some serious training. At a recent Queen's Badge Training Course the candidates were asked to consider these questions:

> Should the Brigade be giving more training for life – for example, on finance (mortgages), fashion, cars, family relationships, alcohol, sex, drugs? If so, how should it be put over?

The Company is part of the Church. In your experience, is this relationship as close as it should be? If not, how can it be improved?

The B.B. Organizer in Nigeria has travelled thousands of miles to visit remote B.B. Companies in the mat-roofed villages. It is harmattan season, the season of dry dusty winds, and the mornings are chilly!

The month of May brings the big-scale Battalion and District events, and the full panoply of the Albert Hall Display. One can be assured that the 2nd Enfield Company will once again put on an outstanding show. Boys of the Senior Section of the 1st Ottawa make a canoe trip on Oplongo Lake and River in the Algonquin Park for a weekend. The Singapore Companies are at camp at Changi, of

Singapore, jungle survival   fateful wartime memory. The most popular activity there is a jungle survival course.

High summer means the joy and adventure of Camp, and countless other outdoor pursuits. One candidate for the Duke Edinburgh's Award makes aircraft his project. He had a detailed record of civil, R.A.F., and foreign types of aircraft visiting his local airport. He has taken and logged photographs of various aircraft observed at air displays. He has flown in a club aircraft for at least ten hours and kept a log of his flying time. He knows something about the aesthetics of aircraft design and international aviation projects.

A new Company is enrolled in Papua New Guinea, and the Boys 'fall in' in traditional style.

Every year more and more teams of enthusiastic Boys take part in a variety of endurance hikes. The annual Cleveland Hike, for example, may have an entry of 300 teams, some of them from as far away as Denmark. The West Lowland Hike takes place over the Cumnock and Muirkirk hills of Scotland with 27 miles to cover and

*London District Display
at the Royal Albert Hall*

'incidents' to endure and overcome at an assault course on the way. The Charnwood Hike, Waltham Walk and Kilbryde Hike set over a thousand young men on a strenuous 48-hour course which involves B.B. tests, scrambling across a river, initiative tests and an obstacle course. It is, in short, endurance hiking against the clock and against constant hazards, carrying full camping gear, safety equipment and rations. Here is the B.B. out-of-doors at its best, with challenge, adventure, fellowship, sense of achievement, and spirited fun for everyone.

Dalguise, in Perthshire, is one of a number of Battalion Outdoor Centres which is a doorway to the open-air world all the year round.

109

Outdoors: Challenge, Adventure, Fellowship

It is a 17th-century Scottish manor house set in grounds of 50 acres
with the Grampians for a horizon, a nearer prospect of moors, lochs
and rivers, and some of the finest forest in the kingdom, full of oak,
pine, fir, red maple, silver birch and larch. Dalguise is leased by the
Glasgow Battalion of The Boys' Brigade as a centre for all manner of
outdoor activities – canoeing on the River Tay, archery, orienteering,
rock-climbing on the sheer faces at Craig-y-Barns, skiing on the slopes
of Ben Lawers or Glen Shee, pony-trekking, swimming and
water-skiing, learning to handle a dingy on Loch Tay, hill walking
and camping. It is heaven on earth for adventurous Boys.

For the challenge of the Duke of Edinburgh's Award there are six gold standard expeditions – on Dartmoor, in the Peak District, North Wales, the Lake District, and two in the Cairngorms.

All B.B. Activities make great demands on the Officers and Instructors, whether their work lies in the back streets of grey cities, in scattered rural districts, or up and down the exotic islands and tropical lands far round the world. Wherever they serve, they remember the words of the Founder:

> An Officer can never afford to forget that the Brigade is made up of Companies, and that his own Company is for him the most important and supreme bit of work that he is called upon to do.

And wherever they meet, indoors and outdoors, generation after

generation of Boys learns to sing of the emblem that binds them all together:

> There's an emblem fair that is known to all,
> a sign to help us through;
> It stands for strength and it stands for right,
> An Anchor tried and true.
> The emblem of The Boys' Brigade it helps us on our way
> Our fathers knew in days gone by the sign we know today.

CHORUS:

> Sure and stedfast, the Brigade Boys' motto clear
> That's our watchword when troubles and trials are near.
> Sure and stedfast, to the flag that flies above
> In all that we do we'll try to be true to the Anchor
> that we love.

The Boys' Brigade is the first of all uniformed youth movements to reach its 100th birthday. Thousands of Boys and Officers in its Glasgow birthplace and throughout the United Kingdom and all round the world celebrate the day they are a century young.

1983 is the year to look back and to look forward. For the B.B. it begins on the other side of the world with an International Camp for more than two thousand Boys at Mystery Creek, Waikato, New Zealand, where Christmas and New Year are high summer and the outdoor activities will include horse-riding, fishing, canoeing, sailing and sports of every kind. Will they remember that William Smith of faraway Scotland was the first to think of camping for Boys?

TOMORROW'S MEN

Birmingham Boys with a trophy they won at camp

The Centenary Camp is at Scone Palace, the ancient royal capital in the heart of Scotland. Two thousand Boys and Officers are there to start the main celebration in the sunshine days of August. Seniors, NCOs, Warrant Officers and Young Leaders have their own Campus '83 during the same summer month in the setting of the Cathedral and University of Durham. They come together to enjoy themselves and to celebrate the centenary, but they also look to tomorrow. Many of the young people who attend Campus '83 will be the future leaders of the Brigade and its kindred organizations in the United Kingdom and Europe.

London has its own Royal Gala night at the Barbican Centre as well as the biggest and best-ever Albert Hall Display. In Glasgow a new British Rail main-line locomotive is named 'The Boys' Brigade' to blazon the Movement up and down the land. B.B. visitors in their individual uniforms from every corner of the earth parade the city

116

A happy leap forward

streets for the centenary meetings of Brigade Council and an open-air Display to rival and outshine the panoply of the still-remembered Jubilee. An open-air service at Ibrox Stadium attracts a memorable mass gathering, and the opening of the Casket sealed in 1933 is its most solemn moment. What message did the Boys of the Jubilee Year hand on to the Boys of the Centenary? What have the Boys of the century to say to their young brothers of tomorrow?

Public parks everywhere vie with one another to show the centenary logo in full floral display. Television, radio, and the national and local press take full account of the occasion with news of Boys celebrating their very special birthday. There are relay runs, projects to help others, the planting of trees in commemoration, bonfires, balloons, concerts, and messages sent flying round the globe to tell of The Boys' Brigade and its work for the youth of yesterday, today and tomorrow.

First day covers, 1982

Philatelists everywhere have their first-day cover with the B.B. stamp issued on October 4th, that day of days when the very first Company formed up for the first time in the North Woodside Mission Hall. Also in October thanksgiving services are held in Edinburgh, Cardiff, Belfast and Dublin, culminating in a national service of thanksgiving on the Founder's birthday in St. Paul's Cathedral, London, to bring the official centenary events in the United Kingdom to a close.

The end of one century is the beginning of another. What of the future for The Boys' Brigade? The Boys who take part in the Centenary celebrations inherit not only the ominous year 1984, but look forward to 2000 A.D. and the dawn of a new millennium.

1983 is a good time to take stock. The Old Boys of yesterday remember the good old days of cap, belt and haversack, of drill and Bible class and summer Camp. The Boys of tomorrow may look for something different. They can take heart from the example of the Founder, William A. Smith, who was the most forward-looking man the B.B. has ever known.

The Boys' Brigade has not been in a hurry to change in its first hundred years. But the world about them has changed more in half that time than in all previous recorded centuries. It will go on changing with bewildering speed. The first B.B. Boys of 1883 knew

118

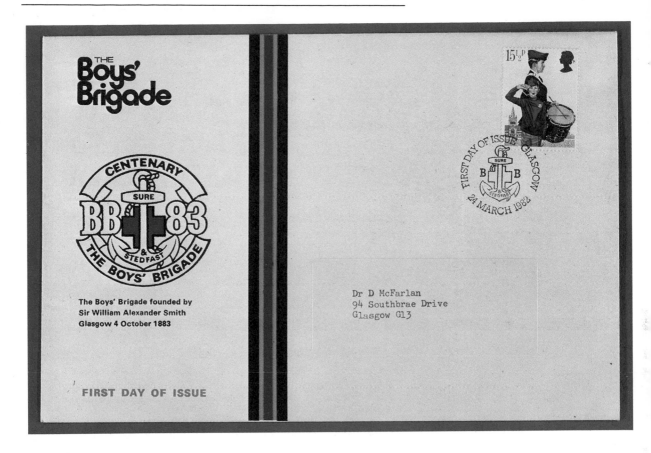

nothing of motor cars or aeroplanes, electric light, pop music, films, radio or TV. They wore 'tackety' boots and loads of stuffy clothing, with wool next to the skin and a celluloid collar for Sunday church parade. What will tomorrow's B.B. Boys plan and do in a microchip and video age?

One may venture a few guesses. Will there be less emphasis on military rank and drill and discipline? In 1893, when the B.B. was only ten years old, someone asked 'What is the Object of The Boys' Brigade?' The reply from a man in the street was 'Being good and playing at soldiers.' It was a ready answer in those imperial days. The first Officers were almost all Volunteers and it was natural to model the Movement on the military forces which proudly policed and garrisoned the Empire. The B.B. uniform, drill, activities and awards have symbolized the military traditions and style. The virtues of the Object, too, 'Obedience, Reverence, Discipline and Self-Respect',

119

Pull for Tomorrow

belong to that heritage. They speak of an age of control rather than of growth and freedom.

The B.B. of tomorrow, surely, must take account of a new style and quality for young life in a new era. Changes are already proposed. Ranks and terms such as 'Private' and 'Colour Sergeant' will disappear. The B.B. stages of tomorrow from age 6 to 17 are to be Anchor Boys, Juniors, Seniors and Cadets. There will be a new badge structure with terms such as leadership, community, physical activity, interests and adventure. It would be an interesting centenary task to invite thoughtful B.B. Boys and their Leaders to write a new Aim and Object in keeping with 1983 and onwards. What ideals for tomorrow in the words of today would they set before their successors in place of the worthy standards of Obedience, Reverence, Discipline and Self-Respect which have served The Boys' Brigade so well throughout their first hundred years?

The most daring idea for the future has been the proposal to admit girls to the membership of The Boys' Brigade. Already The Girls' Brigade has a similar membership, sharing the same headquarters and joining the Boys in such activities as displays, marching-bands, community service, local camps and church parades. But the B.B. was founded to be a Movement for Boys, leading to Christian Manliness. A lot of words and ideas would have to change to bring

Springboard to the future

121

about an entirely new and different organization, and other movements would have to come in to the discussion. Nevertheless, there is bound to be a growing together. Healthy boy-girl relationships are a positive part of any youth work today.

Tomorrow's problems are already here. Family life is not as strong as it was when good Queen Victoria was on the throne. There are ethical challenges to boys and girls undreamed of by their grandparents. There will be fewer Boys in the 11 – 17 age range in the next decade. One-sixth of the youth population will be coloured. The 12-year-old B.B. Boy of the very first Company in 1883 already had a job and a life's work lay ahead of him. Today, the teenager may face unemployment for many uncertain years. It is hard to help Boys to live by Christian values in a mixed and troubled society.

One thing The Boys' Brigade must always remember if it is to be true to itself. It was founded as a Christian organization, and that has been its declared Object through a hundred years. The B.B. belongs to the family of the Church. It is 'Sure and Stedfast' only when Boys and Leaders learn together to honour their motto in personal Christian commitment and service.

The words of the Brigade President are a challenge to the Boys of today and tomorrow:

> Think of the past, be thankful for the present, be immensely
> in hope for the future.

Brigade Presidents

James Carfrae Alston	1885–1909
Rt. Hon. Lord Guthrie	1909–1919
Col. John A. Roxburgh	1919–1933
Rt. Hon. The Earl of Home	1933–1947
Rt. Hon. Lord Maclay (Sir Joseph P. Maclay)	1947–1963
The Earl of Elgin and Kincardine (Lord Bruce)	1963–

Brigade Secretaries

William Alexander Smith	1885–1914
H. Arnold Wilson (Honorary)	1914–1925
G. Stanley Smith	1925–1954
Major-General D. J. Wilson-Haffenden	1954–1965
Ian G. Neilson	1966–1974
Alfred Hudson	1974–